NURSE JACK

TRUE HOSPITAL STORIES, HOSPITAL COVERING UP A RAPE, CRIME, DRUG ABUSE, TRAGIC LOSS, AND COMICAL STORIES.

JACK S HOUSTON

Nurse Jack

Tellwell Talent
www.tellwell.ca

ISBN
978-0-2288-3533-2 (Hardcover)
978-0-2288-3532-5 (Paperback)
978-0-2288-3534-9 (eBook)

Table of Contents

Preface

I am a nurse, a registered nurse to be precise. Throughout my career, working in general hospitals, psychiatric wards, community-based nursing, and prisons, I've heard my colleagues say, "You could write a book about this place," usually after a stressful event that most people wouldn't believe could happen, or would be shocked by if they witnessed it. So, I have been keeping track of these events, with the idea that, maybe when I retire, I will write a book about these very events. And guess what? I did just that.

I have tried to make these stories amusing, but not all of them can be; some are very sad, and some are criminal in nature. One thing that I would like you to remember is that I have always tried to treat my patients with respect, so when I am telling a funny story, please understand that I am not making fun of the patient, even though the story may be humorous. I bear no prejudices whatsoever, but some of the stories I've included are about racism and inequality.

Allied health is a term that refers to all the other professionals, besides the nursing staff, who are involved in the care of patients: licensed vocational nurses, nurse aides, social workers, physiotherapists, and doctors. Notice I did not list doctors first; this is the way a layperson would usually make the list, but doctors are only people, too—some great, some not so great, and some absolutely terrible. You will hear about all these professionals in my stories.

What follows is a sampling of the many stories I have heard and experiences that I have had while working as a registered nurse. Some of the stories are my own and others are those of my co-workers. In all of the stories, the names have been changed to protect the identities of those involved.

I must point out another very important fact: none of these stories, or anything in them, should ever be taken as medical advice; go to your doctor for that. When I refer to medical procedures and lab values, or describe various disease processes, it is only enough to make sure you know what I am talking about so that the story makes sense. There are huge gaps in some cases that would describe the entire illness; these stories are only meant to capture the gist of what happened.

I hope you enjoy these anecdotes I have gathered over my 30-plus years of experience.

I Am Not Gay

I am not gay—not that there's anything wrong with that, as Jerry Seinfeld once proclaimed on his show. I am not in any way prejudiced toward gay people and have both friends and family who are gay. It was never a big deal for me, but before I became a nurse, I had never been asked if I were gay, over and over again.

When I was a young nurse, just out of school, I took my first job in a hospital in Texas. I was blatantly asked many times by people from all walks of life: "So, are you gay?" "You must be gay, are you not?" "Oh, I thought you were gay!" "I'm sorry, I thought you were my nurse, so you must be gay—or are you my doctor?" Can you imagine how you would react to that type of question if it were posed to you repeatedly over your first month at a new job, and you were not gay?

It was a very big surprise to me that in the late '80s and early '90s a vast majority of my patients assumed that if you were a man and a nurse, then you must be gay. Admittedly, there were not a lot of men in nursing at the time in the state of Texas, so I guess people were not used to the idea.

This at first made my job much harder. Many of the patients, especially the elderly women, not only assumed that we male nurses were gay, but they also had it in their heads that we were up to no good, or could not be trusted, as though we were some type of sexual deviants. They didn't easily trust us to look at their genitalia, or, heaven forbid, to change a dressing or insert a catheter. You might assume that if the patient was uncomfortable, we could just go fetch one of the female nurses to do these procedures, but the reality is that we were very often understaffed and there were not always female nurses available to accommodate the patient.

In many cases, these patients' medical conditions meant that they could not wait, and the procedure had to be done in a timely manner. The really strange thing is that so often, when a patient was reluctant to allow us to perform a procedure on her, a male doctor would enter the room and the patient would suddenly open up her legs like they were on a hair trigger. They had no qualms whatsoever about the male doctor's intentions. He could have been a real scumbag, but they would never question his integrity or sexuality. He was a doctor, so everything was OK.

One night shortly after two of us male nurses had been talking about this dilemma, our charge nurse said, "Well boys, you're not going to like this article in today's paper!" She proceeded to read aloud the contents of the article that described a patient who woke up at another local hospital to find that a male nurse was performing fellatio on him. You can bet that made our job extra hard for a couple of months. What more could go wrong?

On one occasion after I had been providing care to an elderly patient for three evenings in a row, and she had asked me daily whether I was gay or not, I became more assertive, telling her that I was definitely not gay, I had a girlfriend, and we were engaged. I believed that she finally understood.

As I was assisting her to the bathroom with her walker, she spontaneously reached down and grabbed my genitals, winking at me, just before her dentures dropped out of her grinning mouth and to the floor.

Many people have heard nurses refer to "that dirty old man" talking about some old guy they had as a patient. I believe that we hear this a lot because, historically, women represented the bulk of the nursing staff, but now that more men are in nursing, we are discovering that some women are also inappropriate, or I hate to say it, but could be referred to as "dirty old women."

I was with another male nurse one night when I observed him say to a female patient, "Well, I understand you may be uncomfortable with a man—or anyone—doing this procedure on you. I wouldn't like to have this inserted in me either, by anyone, let alone a woman, me being a man and all, but if I had to have it, I would."

The woman needed a Foley catheter inserted, by the doctor's orders, PVR (post-void residual). Some people do not empty their bladder enough, which brings a bunch of problems with it. So, after she peed, we had to insert a catheter to see how much urine was left in her bladder. Ideally, less than 50 cc should remain. My colleague Mel explained to the lady, "I will never force this on you, and I will ask for a female nurse to come from another unit to do it, but realistically it will be a long time before anyone comes, and the test will not be accurate, and you will remain distended and maybe uncomfortable for a lot longer than you have to be." He had a gift when talking to people; she agreed to the procedure and everything went smoothly.

Well, things did eventually level out, and, in fact, after the female patients got used to us, they started asking for us by name instead of the female nurses who worked there.

We would often hear patients say to other nurses down the hall, "No, I want Nurse Jack, or Nurse Mel." There is a lot to be said for building trust with your patients—it's paramount.

I do believe that today things are better for men in nursing, but unfortunately, the old stereotype is still perpetuated by enough people that it still is an issue at times. Please stop and think before you make jokes or poke fun at people for the job they have selected. Don't do things to influence young children in developing bias toward people. In today's world, almost any job can be done by either a man or a woman.

I Cried with Her

Men are tough, and women are the weaker sex. This is what used to be said years ago, and what an awful thing to say. There are many things we learn from our elders that we, unfortunately, should never have learned. We men look at women's breasts all the time, even though we have been told by other women—our mothers for one—that women are not objects, or play toys, or to be taken for granted, and we must have respect for women, blah, blah, blah. *It's just Mom worrying about me again,* we think to ourselves, *she's just being oversensitive.* On the other hand, we men see women doing what could be described as showing off their breasts, wearing low-cut tops, no bra, etc., not that I have ever complained.

I believe just as young men learn bad habits, so do young women. Maybe not necessarily bad habits, but they quickly learn that if they have nice breasts, men will certainly pay attention to them. After all, it's only human nature. It's a biological fact that the male species is attracted to a female's breasts. It's part of the big picture of life. Have you ever wondered, though, whether both males and females put too much emphasis on women's breasts? I wish we didn't, and I will tell you why.

When I was all of 20 years old, I was stationed on a medical-surgical floor, near the end of my training, and I was very proficient at things like dressing changes and the like. I had on my patient list a very young female patient, Miss Green, who was post-operative after having had a total right-sided mastectomy. The report I was given was that the incision site had become infected, and I had to change the dressing, note the drainage, color amount, clean the incision, and apply a new dressing. Easy, no problem. I had changed lots of dressings.

I walked into the room to find Miss Green staring out the window with a very sad look on her face, and I could tell right away this was going to be anything but easy, especially for her. After telling her what I was there to do and explaining the procedure, like any good student would do, she said okay. At that time, I took the night table, adjusted it, placed it in a good position to both set my dressing tray on and to be able to reach. All was going well until Miss Green, all of 29 years of age, removed her gown to allow me access to the dressing.

I had to be careful as I removed the dressing, as the tape can often pull skin off with it, and while I was doing this, she asked if I had been working there for long. I knew she was just attempting to make small talk to get through the moment, but I answered her questions as I peeled off the old gauze. When the dressing was off she looked down and then turned her gaze toward the window, where the view was of cloudy skies and rain running down the dirty window, but it was obviously better than the view of her chest, which was now missing an entire breast, and I'm sure, looked very empty and horrific to her.

At that time, I noticed her starting to shake, and she began sobbing, something I'm sure she had been doing a lot and was going to be doing for a while. I remember asking her if she wanted me to give her a moment. She said in a very low, soft voice, "No, please, just do it, I'm okay." She was far from okay, but I proceeded, and as I continued cleaning the wound, I noticed a trail of tears had fallen onto her upper chest and had begun running down toward the wound. I couldn't imagine how this very young woman must feel. She was still single; what must have been going through her head at this point? Having cancer is bad enough, and losing a part of your body is traumatic for sure. But, when it is a woman's breast, it must be that much more so. How would I know? I'm not a woman. But I was there to witness one of the cruelest things a woman should ever have to endure.

Men are naturally drawn to breasts; every woman knows that. Now, this poor girl was missing one. How could any woman take that in stride? This young woman was clearly traumatized; it was one of the hardest things I'd had to deal with at that point. I did not have any way to comfort this woman at the time. I felt horrible about that. I thought I should know something to say, or do but . . . maybe it was best at the time to say nothing, get the job done, and leave her to collect herself.

I myself became overwhelmed with emotion, quite by surprise, because men are the stronger sex, we are tough. Bullshit! As I was cleaning up, I attempted to tell my patient to call me with the buzzer if she needed anything, and my voice began to crack. I cleared my throat and repeated what I had started to say, and had to make a quick exit from the room. I was filled with tears myself, and I couldn't let her see me that way.

I exited her room and went into the dirty utility room to get rid of the soiled bandages, and send the dressing tray back to be sterilized. I was also hiding from the full-time nursing staff because I—a man, you know—was not supposed to tear up over a patient. At that time, one of the older nurses came into the room, and I turned away from her as I said, "I'll be out in a minute—I'm just cleaning up after myself." I then felt her hand on my shoulder, and she said, "Take a few minutes, kid, you'll be okay—that's hard stuff to deal with. We have to be strong, strong for her." She never missed anything; she was a great nurse and a wonderful lady.

The world can be very cruel, but I feel our preconceptions of the way things should be, due to the way we were raised, the experiences we've had, the way we see our dad or uncles act, etc., influence us sometimes, so that patients like Miss Green end up suffering even more, much more than she had to.

I saw her about 12 years later in the grocery line. I never forget a face. Apparently, she remembered mine too. As she came up in line behind me, with who appeared to be her husband, she looked at me and I knew she recognized me. I nodded and said, "Hello." She smiled as she said, "Hello, how are you? Are you still working at the hospital?" I was so very happy to see her doing so well. She looked very happy—and as beautiful as ever.

I Miss That SOB

On a medical-surgical unit, not all patients have surgery and go home a few days later, and not all patients come in and die shortly after. Sometimes, patients are hospital bound for weeks or months at a time, get well enough to go home, and ultimately have to come back in a few months and start all over again, and this cycle can go on for years in some cases.

This was the case with our patient, Ida. When I first met her she said, as she gasped for air, "You know, son, I'm a real SOB: short of breath that is"—she laughed and winked at me as she began coughing and gasping for air again—"although some might say I'm a real son of a bitch, too!" And she began laughing again, followed by that horrifying cough and wheezing. She suffered from very severe COPD, (Chronic Obstructive Pulmonary Disease), and was receiving oxygen through a hose and face mask at the time. Ida was all of 62 when I met her for the first time; she looked 85 if she were a day. Life had treated her hard, and she herself had not been kind to her lungs as I would learn in the months to come through our conversations. "I'm an old barfly, I've been around, I know what's what, I used to have a good time when I was young," she would say as she would give that big wink of hers that we all grew to know was a telltale sign that she liked you and appreciated you. These hospital stays had been going on for about three years.

One time, my co-worker Todd and I were out at the local honky-tonk (that's a country bar for you people up north), when the pretty young bartender brought us both another round and said, "This one's on Ida," and pointed to a frail elderly lady sitting on the other side of the bar with her oxygen tubing on. When we looked her way, she smiled from ear to ear. We naturally went over to say hello, and she hugged us both and said, "There's my two favorite boys in the world," followed by, "Are you having any luck with the girls tonight?" Then, she gave that big wink. After we spoke with Ida for a few minutes, she said, "Well, boys, don't miss your chance. Get after them young ones before they're gone." She was an old barfly for sure. Later that night we were talking about how nice it was to see Ida out enjoying herself like that. After all, we had known her for about three years and spent a lot of time with her, and actually knew her better than some of our own family. You're not ever supposed get emotionally involved with a patient, and you're always supposed to be professional. Even though we were always professional and treated her properly, and never forgot that she was our patient, it's hard for some patients not to grow on you. Ida was just that kind of patient.

About a week later, Todd and I both arrived at work and sat down at the nursing station, waiting for our report from the nurse who had been in charge that day. She said that Ida came in last night and kept asking for the two of us. She kept saying, "Send in Jack and Todd, send my boys in." Just then, as the nurse broke down and started to cry, the funeral home wheeled Ida's body by us both. We, being strong young men, took it in stride for about 30 seconds, and then we had to abruptly leave the area and do what men rarely ever admit to doing—and I am actually doing it now as I'm typing, and that was 30 years ago. I really do miss that SOB, short-of-breath barfly.

Marital Duties

One would think that the people who run a hospital should not only know right from wrong, but be able to recognize a crime and report it immediately when made aware of it.

What are "marital duties"? What does that mean to you? Is it a duty to have sex with your partner whenever they feel the need, no matter what situation you are in at the time?

When I was a very young nurse, barely an adult, I found myself faced with the toughest decision of my life. I had a patient who had been in a coma for several days after an automobile accident. Mrs. Slate was now out of her coma but had what appeared to be significant brain damage. She could speak and recognize people, somewhat. However, it was uncertain how good her memory was and how well she recognized people. She could not answer direct questions or follow instructions. She could, however, recite nursery rhymes.

That part of the brain's memory can sometimes be preserved. She would rock back and forth in her bed while muttering the words to "Mary Had a Little Lamb." I noticed that she would do this more so when she was agitated, or what I believed to be afraid. She required almost total nursing care, and she had been placed in a suite. This is a regular room with a large television and a private bathroom, connected to an adjoining room with the same. It was very costly, but she had great insurance and she was going to be there for a long time. So, she was a very good customer for the hospital.

One evening I was rushing around the unit trying to get all of my work done when I entered Mrs. Slate's room.

I stopped in my tracks and froze for a second as I saw something so incredibly horrid, I had to make sense of it before I could react. What I saw was Mr. Slate rolling off of his wife, who was clearly agitated and rocking back and forth muttering "Mary Had a Little Lamb." Her husband was quickly trying to pull up his trousers, as he was also trying to pull up her diaper and put it back into place. He then yelled at me and said, "We need time to ourselves to take care of our marital duties." I yelled at him, "Get the fuck out of the room, now!" He stood there and argued his case as I took Mrs. Slate's pulse that was running about 140 bpm. In my estimate, she was terrified; I don't believe she even recognized her husband. She was definitely not competent and was in no way fit to make decisions on her own.

I called the nursing supervisor immediately, as well as Mrs. Slate's doctor and my head nurse who was at home. All of these people seemed surprised and informed me what a good job I had done, and that they would have a meeting with Mr. Slate in the morning to rectify this, as well as get him any help that he needed, as he was obviously not able to accept his wife's condition. That was also a possibility that I recognized, but I doubted it was the case. I believed he was just a selfish prick with low morals.

After several hours of charting the incident and filling out incident forms, etc., I finished my shift; Mrs. Slate was safe, and I was leaving work on holidays for the better part of a week. Time off is never enough, especially when you come back to a horrible mess or a shitty work environment where making money is the primary goal of the hospital.

Upon returning from my vacation, I quickly learned that Mr. Slate had continued with his nightly visits with the door shut, while I had been away. The female nursing staff all seemed to think that he was still making his wife perform her "marital duties," as Mr. Slate described it.

I became very angry and began looking through the chart to view the nursing notes and doctor's notes. I could not find anything, no notes, not even my own. The chart had been thinned just prior to me starting my shift. The term "thinning the charts" refers to when a chart becomes so full of paper that no more can be inserted without the rings in the binder failing, and all of the pages falling out. It usually takes several weeks or often months to get to the point that the charts would have to be thinned. So, clearly, there was only one reason to thin the charts before I started back at work, and that was to hide what I had written. I could not believe what I was seeing. I went to the old chart, which is where we put the overflow of charting when a chart needed to be thinned. They were there: all of the notes that I had made—the proof, so to speak. Sadly, I even found evidence that they had performed a pregnancy test on Mrs. Slate and hid it, as well. Thankfully it was negative. At the end of my shift, the day staff and all of the managers came in to work. I insisted we have an emergency meeting on the spot. At one point, as they all seemed to be defending Mr. Slate, the head nurse yelled at me, “It’s not any of your business. It’s his wife. You need to stay out of it.” I then said to her, “So, what you’re saying is that if you have an accident, and wake up out of a coma, and don’t know who your husband is, I should just let him have sex with you whenever he wants, even if it scares the hell out of you.”

That is when she slapped me in the face, in front of all the staff, harder than I had ever been slapped before, as she screamed at me, “Shut your mouth!”

I collected myself and then said, “This is what is going to happen. I am going to the state police and the news, and I will be reporting this today if you do not report it and do the right thing.”

Well, within the next two hours they had not one, not two, but three doctors in to write notes that Mr. Slate was not to be allowed into the room again unaccompanied. They also stated that Mrs. Slate was not competent. They did report it. They also had him assessed and sent for help. I was very inexperienced in life at that time and would certainly handle that type of situation more swiftly now, but at the time I trusted my superiors and the doctors.

I almost lost my job that day, and I might as well have. I was treated very poorly after that and soon quit. It left a bad a taste in my mouth. As time went on, I learned that people turn their heads a lot when it comes to rich people’s requests, or they come out ahead financially by keeping their mouth shut. Sometimes people are just scared to speak up, like I believe each and every one of the female nurses on that unit was. Most people really need their job and know they could easily be fired. I didn't give a shit about my job, so I spoke up. I was compelled to. I was not in any way a hero. I just did what anyone raised the way I was would do. Also, my response would certainly be expected of both the law and the State Board of Nursing guidelines.

My advice to you is this: if you are ever in a similar dilemma, call your lawyer or the police for advice. Don't always trust your superiors will do the right thing. The sooner the problem is dealt with, the sooner you will be able to move forward, as it can eat away at you otherwise.

My Circumcision

Circumcisions are fairly common these days. However, people have different views about both the physical necessity of getting one and the moral issues that surround the procedure. There are some people who, for religious reasons, have this performed on a male baby when the child is still very young. Jewish people celebrate the day and call it a "bris." Other people believe it is a form of child abuse, as you are literally cutting off a piece of the boy's penis. Some people have their child receive a circumcision simply because they themselves had it done. Unfortunately, some people who are not circumcised have difficulties later in life, from a medical point of view, and have to receive a circumcision as an adult. This is something that no man ever wants to do. It makes me tremble just thinking of the prospect of having an operation on the end of my penis. It's a nightmare for most men to think of such a procedure.

When I was just a student nurse, I was doing my obstetrical rotation and had much to learn. Dr. Mallard was on the unit, and was going to be performing a circumcision on a one-day-old baby. The nurse came and got me, so that I could observe and learn from the experience. Dr. Mallard was a pediatrician who had actually been my doctor as a young boy. I was always incredibly afraid of him; this giant of a man would give me a huge needle in the bum almost every time I saw him. To my surprise, that giant from my memory was actually all of 5'2". He had a soft voice, with a unique, unmistakable pitch. He was a very kind man, loved by all.

I had not seen him in at least 15 years but knew him as soon as I heard his voice, it was so distinctive. The nurse led me into the treatment room and introduced me to Dr. Mallard. He looked at me for about two seconds and said, "Now are you Jack? Or the other one, Jeffrey?" I said, "It's me, Jack." It was remarkable how he recognized me now as a young man and not that crying little boy he was used to seeing. I'll never know how he did it. I guess it was my unforgettable good looks.

As Dr. Mallard began the procedure and was placing a clamp on the foreskin to crimp it before he cut off the excess, the nurse began explaining to me that it is best to do the procedure within a few days after birth, as there are better clotting factors with a newborn, etc. She then went on say, "It's hard for some men to watch; it's not easy to see, but when a boy is young, like this, the procedure turns out a lot better, and there is not a big scar, it heals really well."

I, being the super agreeable student, who had been known to, many times in my life, speak before I thought about what I was saying, then said, "Yes, I know. He did my circumcision and it looks great; it's really nice." I was referring to the scar left behind; it just looked the way it was supposed to look, not hideous or anything. Well, didn't the nurse stop mid-sentence, crank her head toward me, and become very red in the face. She was not much older than I was, and she was clearly very embarrassed, as was I.

I then noticed Dr. Mallard's chest shaking as he broke into laughter and said, "That's right, Jack, I did do yours." He continued to laugh, and all I could think was, *I hope he doesn't shake too much and cut the head off this baby's penis*—especially since the mother was a lawyer. He managed to finish the job without incident, and it looked great, no issues at all.

For the next three weeks, that poor nurse could barely talk to me; I think she was still embarrassed. It was not the last time I would put my foot in my mouth. Far from it.

Protect Your Patient and Do No Harm

All medical personnel recite an oath when they graduate. It is often viewed as tradition, or it's just something we have seen in a movie, or heard people talk about. In fact, it is a real thing, and we are bound to it. If you're the patient, I would imagine that you would appreciate that we uphold our oath to do the best we can, to have your best interest in mind when we are caring for you, and to, above all else, not be reckless and hurt you, or make things worse. The actual wording of the oath is much more elegant but that is essentially what it means.

On one particular occasion, an emergency code was broadcast over the PA system. I was one of the six special code team members. When I heard the announcement, I rushed to the emergency room with the expectation that I would soon be performing CPR on a patient, as that is why a code is called the majority of the time.

When I got to the ER, I saw our respiratory therapist Tim standing over a 14-year-old Black male patient, holding a dressing, and applying pressure to the patient's lower abdomen. I would normally expect Tim to be holding a dressing during a code. When we are performing CPR on a patient, it is common to insert a needle into one of the big arteries in the lower abdomen to measure how much oxygen is in the blood. This gives us an idea how effective our procedure or compressions are—basically, if the patient is getting enough oxygen. Tim beckoned me into the room and said, "Jack, can you hold this for me? I need to get into the next room." I said, "Sure," and applied pressure immediately, but quickly noticed that there was a lot of blood, which there should not have been with a routine needle stick/extraction of blood. I said, "Tim, what did you do to this guy?" Tim yelled, "Nothing, he was shot." I finally clued in that I had read the scene all wrong.

As I was applying pressure to the wound, waiting for additional code team members to arrive and assist, Wanda, a nurse I had worked with for several years, rushed into the room and said, "Let me see." She repeated that several times, and then began pulling my hand away, forcibly, which was not good for the patient as he was bleeding profusely. After the third time I yelled at her to stop. When she didn't, I drove her fairly hard in the chest and arm with my elbow, and yelled at her to get out of the room. That's sounds horrible, I know, but she wouldn't stop, and she was harming my patient, getting back to the oath I talked about.

Later, I found out that Wanda had lost her senses because the patient was her own son. I felt pretty shitty at that point, but honestly would do it again to protect the patient. It was then very easy to understand why she behaved as she did—what parent wouldn't?

Tragically, the child was shot with a 9 mm handgun, and the bullet entered his pubic region (lower abdomen) and tracked along the bone, ending up in his thigh down around his knee. I was later informed that bullets often track a bone and follow it. They never mentioned this in nursing school. Unfortunately, the child had suffered severe nerve damage and could never use the leg again.

So, I was able to protect my patient, but no oath can prevent these types of schoolyard shootings when so many kids that age have access to handguns. I strongly feel we are failing both our youth and society with our lax gun laws—or maybe that kid should just not have called the other kid's girlfriend a bitch.

When I was a kid, I did not have access to a handgun and would have just punched the kid in the nose; it would have been dealt with, finished. Times have changed . . . for the worse, I fear.

No Payment Required

There is no such thing as a free lunch, and we all have to pay our bills. Most of us are used to paying with cash, credit card, check, or now online. That's in the everyday world, not in a government institution such as a jail or psychiatric hospital. In this story, the setting is a psychiatric hospital that is also a forensic unit. A forensic unit is basically a medium- to high-security unit, much like a prison, but the people inside are not prisoners, but patients. Generally, people who commit a crime go to jail/prison. When an individual commits a crime but is not capable of making proper decisions, or was determined to be mentally ill at the time of the crime, they end up on a forensic unit. They haven't been given a specific sentence but are on a warrant from the courts, and are to be housed and treated for the illness that they have until they are well enough to go back into society. This does not work for everyone. These people are locked up and taken care of by specially trained hospital staff, often for many years—30 or more, in some cases. They may be there until they die of old age, as they never become fit enough to live in society on their own. This was the case with Jay, a 62-year-old man who had basically lived in an institution his whole adult life.

Jay was a chronic smoker who suffered from schizophrenia, borderline mental retardation (now called borderline intellectual functioning), and had just been diagnosed with COPD, or chronic obstructive pulmonary disease. This meant he had a lot of difficulty breathing at the best of times, let alone when he was smoking. On this occasion, Jay was short on cigarettes as his bartering and trading schemes did not land him enough smokes to get by. Needless to say, he had been in crisis for a couple of days and was having trouble sleeping.

It was the night shift, on a Sunday, about 3:00 a.m., when Jay came to the nursing office. It was difficult to understand him as he was crying like a child, which is not abnormal with his mental state, but it was clear that he had fallen and smashed his face into something. He said it was the night table. He had a large gash in his nose, and there was a nasty flap of skin and deeper tissue, too, hanging off of his nose. I believe he needed stitches, but calling an on-duty doctor was always hit and miss. Some would come right over when called. Some would say just take him to the hospital, which meant calling an ambulance, extra staff, etc. Others would say just let him be seen by the next on-duty doctor. This night, the particular doctor on duty said to apply some Steri-Strips to the wound, and the incoming doctor would look at it in the morning. I'm not sure how drunk the doctor was on that particular night, but Steri-Strips it would have to be. I placed three Steri-Strips on Jay's nose and cleaned him up in the hallway. These strips are basically strips of bandage that are like tape—they hold the skin together like a stitch, but not nearly as well. It's the easy way to close a wound.

Jay had calmed down considerably and began to apologize for crying. He thanked me for fixing his nose, and then went as far as to say, "I owe you. I want to thank you." He then said, "Come on." He was pointing toward his bedroom. When I didn't move, he said, "Come on in, Jack, and I'll give you a blow job. I want to thank you." I quickly told Jay to get to bed, and left the area. Chastising him or disciplining him would have been useless. He was basically trying to pay his debt. Jay, in his mind, was just doing what he had done to pay for things his whole adult life, as well as when he was a child.

In an institution like that, patients learn how to obtain what they need or want by doing sexual favors all the time, especially if they run out of cigarettes. I can't count how many times I have rounded a corner, and witnessed someone "earning" a cigarette. Can you imagine how awful it must be for these individuals when they have to pay their debts? It is absolutely a horrible reality for many, many people in government-run institutions, such as hospitals, jails, and prisons. In this case, there was definitely NO PAYMENT REQUIRED.

Not on My Unit

If you work with people long enough, you get to know how good they are at their job. There was one particular unit on which I worked, where I definitely learned just how competent the staff were. Unfortunately, they were sub-par at best; some might have been described as useless, or even dangerous. You would not have wanted to be a patient under their care.

I broke my leg and had to be admitted to my own unit, as there was not another bed anywhere in the hospital. Just my luck. First, I had to be placed in traction. That was a painful experience, watching three incompetent nurses attempt to set up the traction unit. Physically, it was even worse. The worst thing you can do when you have a fracture is let someone keep moving your leg around, while they try and figure out the harness and weight system.

Later I had three nurses attempt to start an intravenous line four times. It should have been easy as I was young and muscular, and had very easy veins to access. I was not surprised as these three women had usually come to me for help starting their IVs. Most times, after three unsuccessful attempts on a patient, we ask another nurse to try. In my case they were on their fifth try.

At that point I raised my voice and said, “Give me the needle.” I inserted the needle into my own vein; I could have almost done it in the dark. Once the needle was in place I said, “Can you tape it down for me?” They did manage to do that.

I called one of my boys that I ran with and told him I was not able to make it out honky-tonkin’ that night as we had planned. I should not have been surprised to see all the boys show up for a visit to my hospital room, but I was just the same. After all, they were Texans—”never leave a friend behind”—kind of like the Marines.

They didn’t bring flowers, but they did bring three pizzas and two cases of beer. They also showed up after visiting hours, and would have normally been kicked out, but being an employee brought some perks, at least. That was almost 30 years ago, and I still remember the night well. I’ll never forget the smile on my friend John’s face as he entered the room, holding the two cases of beer. He said, “Hey, you crippled fucker, we thought we should come in and see how you’re doing.” His expression was full of mischief.

They had a lot to drink but were quiet and fairly respectful of the noise level in the room. I was on pain medication, so did not drink any alcohol myself and was already a little loopy. I must have drifted off to sleep, as I do not remember the boys leaving.

I awoke to the lovely voice of the head nurse at 7:00 a.m. "What in the hell went on in here last night? You should be ashamed of yourself. You know better than to behave like this. Your friends are not allowed back in this hospital—this is pathetic."

I was still groggy and a little out of it with all the pain meds I was on. She left the room. Although Monique was usually hard to get along with, she had a point.

As I looked around the room, I saw the three pizza boxes lying open on the floor in the corner, beer cans on chairs, tables, the floor, and a nice pyramid of about twenty empty Miller Lite cans stacked on the windowsill. All I could smell was booze. It was disgraceful, but I will never forget my friends and the way they stuck by me, and still do.

I did ask them to never show up with booze again at the hospital. That was received with a big laugh.

He Be Chillin'

When a family member has a significant health condition, we should, whenever possible, learn as much as we can about that condition and accompany them to the hospital if they take ill. Take a moment and ask yourself: How much do you know about the health concerns of each of your family members? Could you speak on their behalf if required?

One afternoon at around 3:00 p.m., I was taking a report from the dayshift nurse prior to starting my evening shift. In a hospital it is routine for one nurse to explain to the next nurse coming on duty, what important things happened with each patient on the shift they were just finishing.

Gerome was giving me his report on a 74-year-old male who was a Type 1 diabetic. This means he was dependent on insulin injections to regulate his blood sugar. Without the proper amount of insulin, the patient could easily die.

Gerome's report went something like this: "This guy's been really agitated and confused. This morning at shift change, he was fightin' with us pretty hard and he ended up pulling out his NG tube. He's been kickin' and thrashin' around, most of the earlier part of the shift, and squealin'."

A nasogastric tube is used to feed patients when they can't eat by themselves for various reasons. It is a tube inserted down the nose and into the stomach of a person. This particular hospital had a rule that an X-ray had to be taken to confirm the proper placement of the tube, as sometimes it could accidently be pushed down the wrong pipe and into the lungs. If a person has a bolus of food pushed down into their lungs, they could die. So, until the X-ray had been done and confirmed to be in the correct location, the patient could not be fed.

Gerome continued on with his report: "So I called for an X-ray this morning but they haven't done it yet. Anyway, he be quiet the last few hours; he's sleeping now. He gets his Humulin 70/30 insulin 30 units in the a.m. and again at supper. That's all you should have to do for this guy. He's quiet now, he's good. He just be chillin' right now."

After Gerome's report, I started my day's work. I entered Mr. Smith's room with my Accu-Chek machine, which is how we measure how much sugar is in the blood. This is necessary to make sure we give the proper amount of insulin, add a little extra sometimes, or hold off if a patient's sugar is too low. The normal amount of blood sugar is 79-110mg/dL. Mr. Smith's wife said to me as I was taking his blood sugar, "I'm, getting worried about him; he hasn't awakened all day. He needs to wake up and eat soon."

Mrs. Smith was correct; he did need to wake up—and soon. His blood sugar was 18mg/dL, and he was unresponsive. He didn't wake up even with me yelling at him and shaking him. I even performed a sternal rub—this is when you push you knuckles hard into someone's sternum and do a twisting motion. It's what you may have seen on TV when a doctor pronounces someone dead. Even if a patient is unconscious, or in a deep sleep, this sternal rub will make them wince; you can see their eyes, they almost squint when reacting to the pain. It is almost a guarantee that if you walk up to one of your friends and do this to them, they will punch you in self-defense—it really hurts. Anyway, Mr. Smith did not wake up and punch me, as he was almost in a coma.

So, looking back on the day, he pulled his NG tube out at 7:00 a.m. and breakfast was at 8:00 a.m. He also received his morning insulin to help deal with the food from breakfast that he never actually had. Also, he had no lunch, nothing to eat all day, as his X-ray to confirm tube placement had not yet been done. Was there any wonder that his blood sugar was so very low?

At that point, I quickly ran to the crash cart and got a large syringe of D50 (this is a pre-filled syringe of sugar water that is used when a diabetic is crashing, or has extremely low blood sugar levels). I injected the syringe—which is quite large in volume, so it takes a couple of minutes—right into a vein in his arm. Before I was done with the injection, Mr. Smith started to mumble something, and by the time I was finishing up, he was talking to us. It still amazes me to this day how quickly a person can respond to that treatment so fast.

It's a good thing that Mrs. Smith was worried about her husband and mentioned it to me; however, it would have been much, much better if she would have known to speak up sooner in the day. If I had started at the other end of my patient list, he might never have awakened. I'm not saying that what I did was heroic; it was just standard procedure for any nurse, no biggie, but it should have never come to that. I couldn't shake the thought: What the hell was Gerome thinking?

Don't ever assume that a health care professional is always doing everything correctly and that everything is under control. I don't mean to suggest that everyone is incompetent, but people do make mistakes. Sometimes they just have a lot on their mind, have way too many patients to care for properly, which is the most common cause for error. Everyone makes mistakes or fails to see the whole picture from time to time; I've certainly made my share of errors. So, don't ever feel intimidated, or that you're wasting a nurse's time. If you think something is wrong, be heard, speak up. In most cases the nurse will give you an explanation to address your concerns, or sometimes they will end up thanking you for pointing out a problem.

He's Just a Mexican

There are many types of nursing jobs that a person can do, one of which is home nursing. Many words are used to describe this type of nursing, often depending on which hospital or company you work for. Regardless of the name, what a home health nurse does is go from one person's residence to another, all day long. Once there, the procedures vary greatly, from doing simple med reviews, checking blood pressure and changing out Foley catheters to administering intravenous medications. It is amazing, some of the things you see when you enter into a person's personal residence. It can be unbelievable, at times very dangerous, and sometimes very, very, sad.

For about a year, I worked a home health job in the state of Texas. The first week on the job, I was sent out to an elderly African-American woman's house to remove a hep-lock that the discharge nurse had failed to remove before the patient left the hospital. A hep-lock is a port that can be accessed intravenously when needed. It looks like a little piece of rubber, the width of a pencil eraser, but has a hole in it that a needle is inserted into, to hook up a line into a person's vein. It is very easy to take out—you just remove the tape and pull. So, I was in and out fairly quickly that day.

When I left the lady's home, there was a group of about 15 young Black teenagers who circled around me and started yelling obscenities. They were calling me a "cracker," "honky," and other choice words. Not only were they yelling verbal obscenities, but most of them had either a bat or an axe handle, and started striking the ground, hard, about six inches from my feet. At one point, a splinter hit my leg. Although I was more frightened than I had ever been, I kept walking and got into my truck. They didn't hit me, but if I had said anything, anything at all, I believe they would have beaten me with their clubs. I could barely drive I was trembling so much, but I managed to make it home safely.

The next day, when I went into the office, I reported what had happened to my co-workers. The other nurses seemed surprised, but when I mentioned where I had been, they said, "No wonder, you were on the wrong side of the tracks—you should never have been sent there." What I learned that day was that the Black people lived on the west side of the railway tracks, and the Caucasians on the east side. The railway tracks were literally the dividing line between the white people and Black people in that town. It was amazing to me that it was actually true, people being divided by a rail line.

At that point, I succumbed to carrying my pistol with me on my rounds, like the rest of the nurses did. Apparently, a number of nursing staff had been held up or robbed, as people assumed we were carrying narcotics with us to deliver to the patients, which we did at times, but rarely. A pistol would not bother the patients, as the large majority of them answered their door holding either a pistol or a shotgun. It was just the norm in Texas.

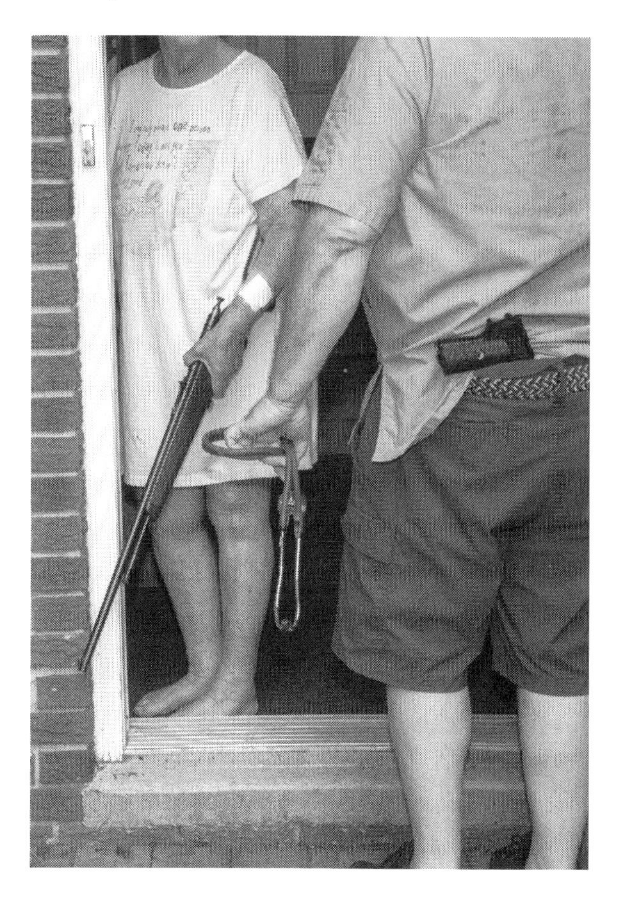

Sometimes, in home health care, you get to know patients very well, as you see them, in certain cases, every week. They begin to enjoy your company and look forward to the visit, not just for the medical care, but to visit with you. Texans are known to be very welcoming people—once they get to know you, or like you. Often, patients would have a meal ready for us, or a to-go bag of cookies or muffins. We were not supposed to take anything from patients, but sometimes it was hard to refuse. They would be hurt if you refused to take their freshly baked bread home with you—and you wanted to because it tasted great. One elderly lady was always giving me plants from her garden to transplant at home. Patients like that made the job enjoyable, not because of the free cookies, but because they were so grateful for the care we gave them. As a nurse, the human factor comes into play sometimes; you can't avoid it, which is great. However, not all of our visits were as pleasant.

I remember going to a new patient's house. I read the address, found the place, and knocked on the door of what appeared to be a 5000-square-foot mansion. It was a beautiful estate. A woman of about 45 years of age opened the door and said, with a look on her face that made me think I was annoying her, "He's in the back, in the trailer; it's my father-in-law you want." She then slammed the door. *What a bitch,* I thought to myself.

As I walked around to the back of the house, I could feel the sweat running down my temples and gathering on the small of my back; it was another very humid day, with a temperature of 103 degrees, a typical day in Texas. Behind the house was a very small steel-covered trailer about eight feet in length, and rounded on both the front and back, kind of like a teardrop shape. I knocked on the door and an elderly woman opened it. She was very polite and greeted me with a smile, saying, "You must be here to help my husband with his medication."

"Yes, Ma'am," I said, then I stepped up into the oven-like trailer, which I was too tall for; I could not even stand up straight in it, and I was a towering 5'6" tall. I saw her husband sitting on the edge of the bed/kitchen table. He also greeted me with a smile and was very polite. He was sitting without a shirt on, sweating profusely as there was no air conditioning, just a little fan. He had already had his left arm amputated as it had been full of cancer. He also had numerous tumors visible throughout his trunk area. He was obviously in a lot of pain, which was why I was there; I had to change out his morphine pack which was hooked up to a pump. It provided a steady amount of pain medicine, and also allowed him to press a button to receive a little more if he needed it for breakthrough pain. It was a PCA (patient-controlled analgesic) pump.

After I had finished replacing the empty bag with a new full bag of morphine, I spoke with the couple for a while. I learned that they had been living in that little sweatbox of a trailer, parked behind their son's house, for the last six months. They had lost their house paying for his cancer treatment, and luckily, his son let them live there in the trailer. I also learned that the son and his wife had no children, just one big-ass house. They were very rich. I could not even imagine what family dynamics had led to this, allowing your dying father to live with your mother in a cockroach-infested trailer, with no air-conditioning, when you had all that space in the mansion. From the way the daughter in-law had greeted me, I thought she might have something to do with it. At any rate, I felt very bad for this man, my patient, and his wife, who had just offered me a cold lemonade. They barely had a pot to piss in, yet they were offering me lemonade and being ever-so courteous. Life can be cruel at times . . . really fucking cruel, from what I had seen that day alone.

Later that day, I arrived at my last visit of the day. It would take a while as I had quite a list of things to do for this fellow. He was an elderly man of Mexican origin, he was dying, and I was told he may not be conscious when I got there, as he had been sent home to die. Well, he in fact was not conscious, and did not have long to live, in my estimate. I had to feed this man through the gastrointestinal tube that was inserted into his stomach, then restart an intravenous line that was no longer patent. I also had to insert a Foley catheter, as the patient was incontinent. As I was doing all of this, three young men, or teenagers, were sitting on a couch at the other end of the room, drinking beer and smoking marijuana. His wife was working in the kitchen, and I noticed a baby crawl across the floor, wearing only a diaper and crying. The floor was so dirty that a path through the dirt could be seen as the baby moved across the floor. I shook my head in disgust.

Last on my list of things to do for my patient was to apply a DuoDERM dressing to the decubitus ulcers he apparently had on his buttocks and hips. People who are bedridden and can't move for themselves often develop skin breakdown, like a dead area of the skin that rots away. I rolled him over to see the decubitus areas and was faced with four of the largest craters that I have ever seen. They were about three to four inches in diameter, and about a half inch deep. He was covered in feces, but the worst part of all were the large cockroaches that crawled out of his wounds. I had never seen that before and I almost puked right on top of the man. The cockroaches were running everywhere. One ran across my forearm, and I nearly had a fit. I was not only sickened by what I saw, but also enraged, as those lazy bastards that I had seen sitting there getting high on the couch could obviously care less about their father. I packed up when I had finished dressing his wounds and left ASAP.

I went home after that, to my apartment, and got out of my truck, walked right past my doorway and to the pool, stripped down to my underwear, and jumped in. I wanted to let the chlorine kill any bacteria that may have been on me. I did not want to wait to get to the shower. It was almost impossible to feel clean after that; it was definitely time for a beer, or two.

The next day I went into the office and informed the nurse in charge of what I had witnessed, and was asking her what exactly we had to do to report such a case of neglect, as the man was in a horrible situation and we were obligated to report such things to the authorities. To my disbelief, she told me, "Don't worry about it, he's just a Mexican." I immediately blew up and started yelling as I threw a chart across the room. I asked her, "What the fuck did you just say?" And she immediately knew I was extremely angry and started waving her hands back and forth as if she were erasing what she had just said. She then said, "No, no, no, Jack, I didn't mean it like it sounded. I just meant that we've already reported that family a couple of times, but when they are Mexican, the authorities know that it's pretty much a waste of time—you're not going to change his situation, as sad as it sounds."

I was still fuming, but the really sad thing is I believed what she had told me. Still, it was difficult to accept the truth, that nobody could do anything for him. I was pissed and was going to talk to the authorities, whoever that was, the next day. Shortly after that I got a call at home to say the man had died. I said I still wanted it looked into, and the supervisor said that she would put in another complaint. That did it for me: I quit that job and never went back to treating patients in their homes. It was too much for me to take. At least in a hospital, patients are seen by many professionals around the clock and cases of gross neglect aren't nearly as common.

Control Your Pets

I am not a huge animal fan by any means, but I don't hate all pets. I do not like it when people let their dogs run wild and jump up on me with mud on their paws. People often say, "It's okay, he's really friendly, he won't bite." In their mind that makes everything okay, like leash laws were never invented. When you're in a patient's home, however, it is a different matter. One has to accept that there will be pets. The problem is that they are not always friendly—and sometimes they are too friendly.

I was making a house call one day at an elderly patient's home. He was a cancer patient and had previously had a port-a-cath inserted into his chest. It is a port or hollow drum-shaped device that is inserted just under the skin, and can easily be accessed with a needle to either inject medicine or draw blood samples, etc. On the other side of the port leading into the patient's vein is a tube with three small separate tubes inside it.

I had only ever accessed a port-a-cath on one other occasion. It was not that difficult, but did have a specific series of steps that had to be performed in the correct order. Also, when performing this task, one uses a specialty port-a-cath tray or kit that comes with all of the supplies needed. I only had one in my box of supplies, so if I messed it up I wouldn't be able to perform the treatment I had come to do. I believed I was up to the task, and I felt as though I could remember how to do the procedure, but I had stopped to run through it in my mind before I entered the residence. Just in case, it always pays to practise the steps in your head, I find.

The patient's wife met me at the door with a smile and invited me in. She led me into her husband's bedroom and said, "There he is." *Not a big talker,* I thought, but I proceeded to unravel my port-a-cath tray, while making small talk with Mr. James. I had not been informed that he was actually suffering from some form of dementia. Initially, I couldn't tell, but soon found out. As I was beginning the procedure, which means inserting a needle into his port-a-cath through the layer of skin in his chest wall, he began to hit me with his fists. He probably did not appreciate what I was doing, and to his credit, he didn't know me. He was probably wondering who this strange man was standing in his bedroom, stabbing him in the chest with a needle. He must have been terrified.

Anyway, when he began fighting me, I tried to calm him down, block his punches with one hand and protect the sterile field that I had laid out on his chest. Also, I did not want the needle to come out of his chest and hurt him or myself. I called to his wife who was sitting in the corner, knitting a blanket, I think. Just at that time, their little dog began to bark, and I thought: *Oh shit, it's protecting its owner, and it's going to try and bite me.*

Luckily, the dog didn't bite me—but the little bastard did start humping my leg. I couldn't do anything but call for help. I was fending off punches from the patient and trying to protect him and myself from the needle in his chest, and balancing on one leg while trying to shake the dog off my other leg. He was really jamming his little pecker into my leg hard. I was being sexually assaulted by a dog. I called again to the wife, who looked up at the scene playing out in front of her and smiled and just continued to go about her knitting. Big fucking help she was.

This dog was out of control and I was not going to stand there until he finished. I had no luck shaking my leg, so I drew back my leg like a football kicker and made a kicking motion as hard as I could. That little bastard missed a stroke and lost his grip then went flying through the air and hit the closet door about ten feet away, where he slumped to the floor. He whimpered and limped to the other room.

The drama was not over yet: I was still battling Mr. James, who had turned into Muhammad Ali. His wife was still knitting and smiling at me. It was almost like something out of a Chevy Chase movie. I finally finished with Mr. James, who calmed down as quickly as he had got all fired up. Neither he nor his wife were firing on all cylinders. It was really sad, but I was not sad to leave that house.

When I left through the front door, Mrs. James let the dog out. He barked at me all the way to my truck but did not try and hump me again. As I was getting into the truck, he did piss on my tire and growl a bit. I must admit I was tempted to run over the little bastard, but didn't. I did wash my leg as soon as I got back to the office. The other nurses really enjoyed my recap of the day.

So, in the future, if any of you have a home visit from a nurse to help you or a family member, please don't let your dog hump the nurse. I assure you they will appreciate you for it.

Do Not Resuscitate

A lot of people will say to their family members things like, "If I'm in a bad car accident and am left with no quality of life, let me die." Well, simply saying so doesn't cut it. If you think that is what will happen, you are in for a surprise. Often, when a tragic accident happens—or a stroke, heart attack, etc.—family members have very differing opinions about what should happen to a loved one. Do Not Resuscitate orders were designed to give medical staff a clear directive as to what a patient's wishes are, if such a need arises and the patient can't speak for themselves.

"Advance directives," for outside of hospital, is another term you may have heard. Advance directives are papers that people fill out, either before a witness or, in most cases now, a notary public, who then places their seal on the document for a small fee—and many will do this for free. A person can even get a bracelet, like a medical alert, for their wrist, depending on the country or state they live in. This makes it easy for an ambulance driver to immediately be aware of the patient's wishes and not to administer excessive life-saving techniques against the patient's will. So, if all of these things are filled out, then there shouldn't be any problems if a person falls ill and can't express their wishes, right? WRONG. Even if you have put a lot of effort and thought into planning for the worst case scenario, often things do not go as planned.

Many times, when someone falls ill, there are family members within the immediate nuclear family who will not agree when it comes to signing a Do Not Resuscitate order. If there are five children involved in making a decision about signing the DNR, at least one of them is usually not ready to let go of the parent. I have seen this many times; one of the siblings will disagree with the others who have already signed the DNR. Then things can get really dicey. There can be threats toward the other siblings. I have seen nursing staff who witnessed the signing of the DNR be put through hell, as the one dissenting sibling threatens to sue the nurse, and then watches every move the nurse makes, eventually demanding that the nurse not be allowed to look after their parent, and demanding that the patient be moved to another floor. Restraining orders have even been put in place by family members in an attempt to keep another family member away from them while their loved one is in hospital. It can become a very big mess, even if everything is done correctly by the staff involved.

Some hospitals will not necessarily honor paperwork that a person has filled out in advance, if it is not to their liking. Lawsuits have been launched against hospitals in the past by disgruntled family members. This is why, in a situation like this, the hospital usually demands that a DNR, with the hospital letterhead and witnessed by their staff, be signed. Sometimes, family members will agree on only certain things to be done to save one's life. For example, if a person came into hospital with sepsis and could be given a bunch of antibiotics to take care of the infection, they would be okay with that. However, if the patient's condition declined further and they needed to be placed on a ventilator, the family might consider that too extreme, and not agree to it. Often, people will agree to many treatments and just say no to the act of performing CPR. Every variable presents an opportunity for family members to disagree. This is why many people fill out Power of Attorney forms ahead of time that allow one particular family member to make these decisions, and these are legal documents and must be followed. But they, too, can be contested in the right circumstance. An example could be if one sibling were to take their mother to a lawyer to have these papers filled out, knowing that they could manipulate the mother into doing so due to her recent onset of dementia. Such children do exist; they get the paperwork completed and sit back and wait for an opportunity to cash in on the old girl's wealth. Then, every time she coughs or gets a hangnail, they're ready to rush her to the hospital. Sadly, this happens, and it can be grounds for a review of the paperwork.

I remember one time standing outside a patient's room many years ago, and listening to the children arguing. I had already read in the report that the children did not all agree about how their father's treatment should go. In this case, the majority of the children had decided NOT to sign a DNR. In other words, they wanted their father to live and to receive all of the care necessary to make that happen. One son, however, was not in agreement. I remember him raising his voice and yelling at his sisters, "He won't be around for much longer, and he's got $600,000.00 worth of Chevron stock going down further every day. Why won't you sign the fucking DNR?"

I could not believe what I had just heard; this guy actually wanted his father to die because the stock his father owned was falling in price, and he wanted to get his hands on it, sooner rather than later, to cash it in. This guy clearly needed a punch in the mouth, but I could not very well do that in front of so many witnesses, so I waited until he went to the parking lot and beat the shit out of him. No, I didn't do that, but honestly, the thought did go through my head. I did, however, say out loud, from the doorway, "A DNR does not have a specific clause in it that deals with Chevron stock." It was all I could come up with in the moment—not the most clever thing I have ever said—but it got the point across that he was being a real asshole, not only to his father, who probably did not have long to live, but also to his siblings. Losing a parent is horrible and life-changing for most people; this man's son was clearly uncouth and—to put it mildly—a selfish prick.

Although a lot of negative things can happen with DNRs, the majority of the time, they are actually very beneficial. Once the papers have been signed, it takes the onus off of the individual family members as things change with one's care, or condition. They are a good thing for most families. I have used such an order with my own family, and it especially took pressure off of me, as siblings often turn to the nurse in the family to make all the quick decisions, thinking that we are supposed to know everything. Let me tell you, when it is our own family member's life on the line, all our knowledge seems to go out the window, because when the strong emotions that accompany the death of a parent are present, it is normal to start second-guessing yourself.

The best advice I can give you is to talk these things over with family members ahead of time, before it is too late—and I mean all the family members who will be involved. Don't leave anyone out; it will ultimately cause added stress and confusion.

Doctor Desperado

All classes of people have people within them who struggle with addiction. It is not something that just the poor, underprivileged, those living in the ghetto, or rich, privileged and entitled kids have to face. There are addicts within every group of people, and medical staff are not an exception.

Many co-workers with whom I have worked over the years have had both drug and alcohol addictions. Many years ago, in the mid '90s, I was employed at a general hospital with a lot of medical and surgical patients. Surgical patients, most of all, require a lot of pain medication, especially in the recovery phase after their surgery.

In the course of those four years, I witnessed the police come onto the unit and arrest five different nursing staff for drug-related offences.

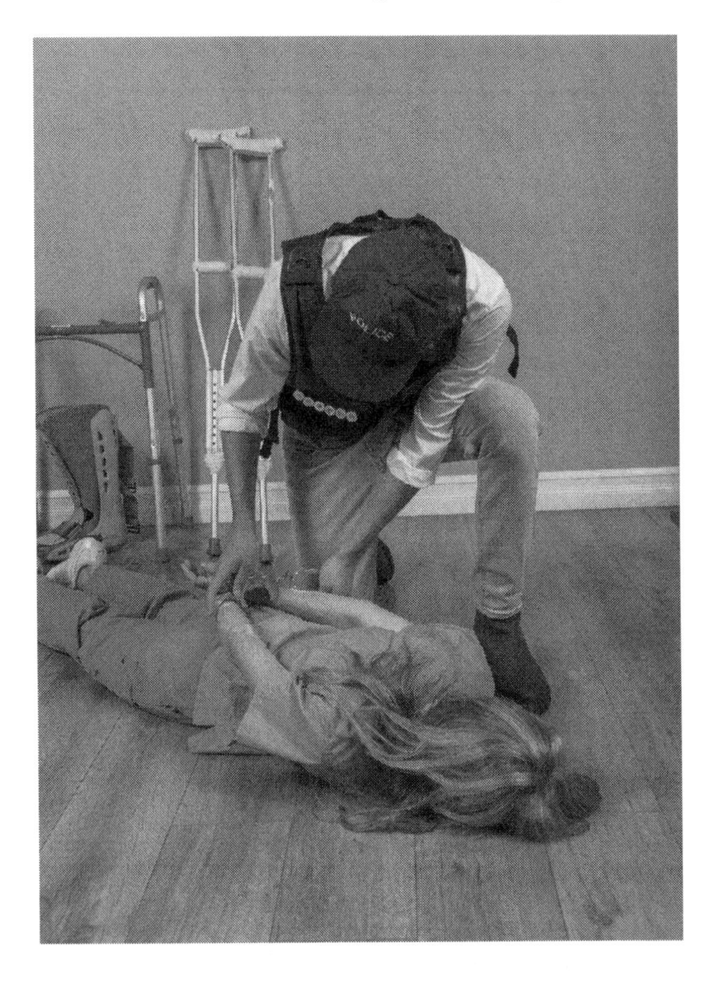

One day, one of the nursing aides said to the RN, Janis, whom she was working with, "Oh Janis, you're bleeding, you have blood on your scrubs," and she proceeded to point to Janis's white scrubs that had a red spot on her gluteal area, right where we give intramuscular injections to our patients. Three of us were there, watching, as Janis looked down and noticed the blood that had been running down her leg from the shot of Demerol she had just injected into her own rear. It was not that uncommon. An addicted nurse would sign out a narcotic for one of their unconscious patients, or someone who was not able to speak for themselves, then they would either put the drugs in their pocket to take home for later or, as in Janis's case, go into the patient's room, drop their drawers, and inject the narcotic into their own hip right there. When Janis realized that she had been caught, she immediately broke down and admitted to it. It turned out that she had had a problem with drug addiction for quite some time. Maybe she wanted to be caught, or at least she needed to be. Can you imagine a nurse looking after you while sneaking your pain medication or someone else's? It's a pretty scary prospect.

On another occasion, Nurse Rose, who I had thought was a pretty good nurse and a hard worker, ran into a little trouble. She had a patient who was a post-hip replacement, and she called his doctor to get an order for pain medication for him: Demerol every three hours for pain via intramuscular injection. She fabricated the order. A nurse is allowed to call a doctor by phone and receive an order and then write it down (e.g., DEMEROL Q4H PRN 50 MG IM VERBAL ORDER/DR. HERNANDEZ/NURSE ROSE), date it and sign the order. So, basically, we are signing our name to the order that the doctor has verbally given us over the telephone. There has to be a certain amount of trust to these things. The doctor may not be in for two or three days to check on the patient. Obviously, the nurse has to know what they're doing. Nurses know a lot more than most people think we do. We are also highly trained professionals.

Sadly, all the training in the world did not help Rose. When addiction comes into play, people often drop the ball and make very poor decisions. About a week after Rose took this order from Dr. Hernandez, one of the other nurses noticed that the patient, who was four days post-operative, had not received anything for pain the previous two nights, but every three hours, at night, for the three consecutive nights before that, then nothing for two nights when Rose was off, and then again every three hours for two nights when Rose was on. To add to that, the patient only used pain meds once or twice during the day when he was active and receiving physiotherapy. It just did not add up. To top it all off, while the head nurse was investigating this odd chain of events, she noticed that the order Rose had received was purportedly from Dr. Hernandez, who was in fact the patient's doctor, but Rose hadn't known that another doctor was covering for Dr. Hernandez, as he'd taken an emergency leave of absence. Rose had an addiction problem, and now she had a legal problem and employment issue, too. She would most likely lose her nursing license, and do a little time as well in the county jail.

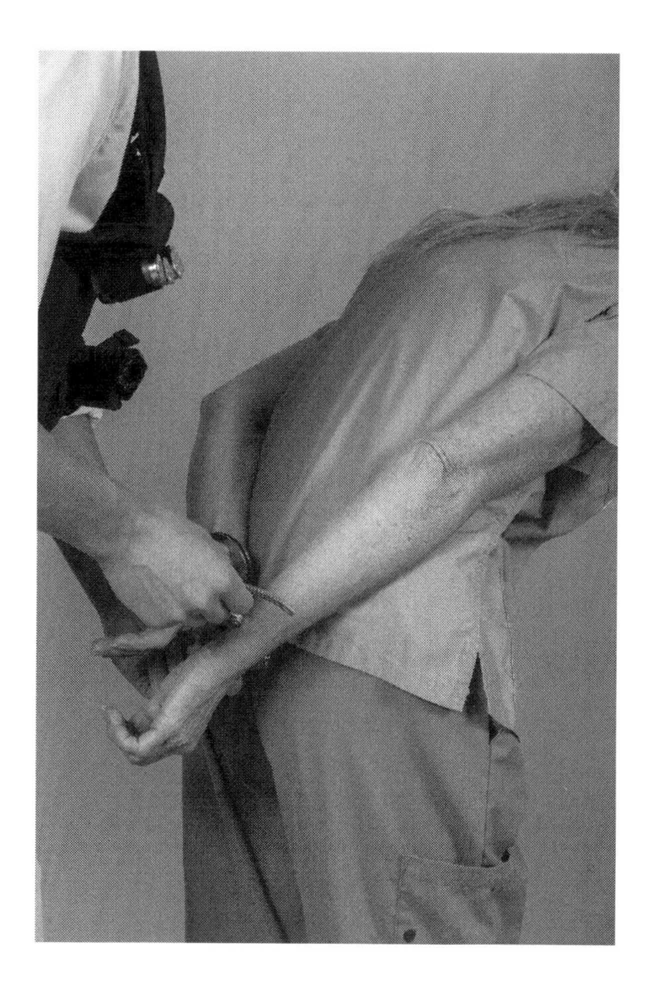

Dr. Cook was one of the nicest guys you would ever want to meet. He was an average-looking white guy, about 5'10" tall and 40 years of age. He was a doctor in the United States, young and healthy, so he should have had the world by the ass, as the saying goes. Everyone liked him; he would spend way more time with his patients than most doctors and not charge them any extra. He would also treat patients and not charge them at all. These were usually Mexicans, as they frequently did not have any insurance. They would show up at the hospital and ask for Dr. Cook, who always greeted them with a smile.

Knowing what I knew about this doctor, and by the way I have described him, you can imagine that what happened next took all of the staff by surprise. One Saturday afternoon, he came barreling through the double doors of the emergency room on his Harley. We were all quite shocked. He smashed through the doors hard, lay the monstrous bike down, and ran into the washroom where he flushed a bag of drugs down the commode. A few seconds later, the police arrived, threw him to the floor face-first, and cuffed him.

Apparently, he had a drug problem that none of us knew about. It certainly wasn't reflected in his work, and he was such an awesome doctor who treated everyone with the upmost respect; yet, his habit had gotten so out of hand that he ended up in such an embarrassing mess. It makes me wonder how desperate he must have been. You just never know what drives people to start using. Anybody, in any group of people, has the potential to become addicted to narcotics, prescription drugs or alcohol. It all depends on what chain of events takes place in their lives. Remember when giving someone a second chance to be very, very careful while doing so. But it is the human thing to do.

Confidentiality

Confidentiality is something that is paramount in all medical disciplines. It is not only important to help build and maintain a therapeutic relationship with patients, but it is also the law and required by each and every regulatory body; this includes nursing, physiotherapy, dentistry, occupational therapy, psychiatry, and all the rest. Can you imagine if we did not keep our confidentiality? Could a patient ever really trust us, knowing we could talk about all their problems out on the street? It would also mean some people would not fully disclose their personal health information, which could adversely affect the outcome of their treatment. These are the reasons that names and identifying factors in my stories have been changed, and even the specific hospitals have not been identified. I have changed enough details in the stories to keep people's identities safe and to not incriminate anyone, while still enlightening you as to the kinds of things medical staff and patients are sometimes subject to. At times, however, it can be very hard to not break confidentiality.

It was the start of what would be another long weekend: a hot and humid summer afternoon in the South. But I was inside the nice, air-conditioned hospital, where things often got much hotter—and harder to bear. I began my day by receiving report from the outgoing shift, followed by making a quick round to look in on each patient. As I was the head nurse, I was running the ship, so to speak, and one of my jobs was to review all new blood work and antibiotics that patients were on, and to compare the culture results, making sure that patients were on the correct medications. While reviewing Mr. Derby's file, I found a note that he had received his first dose of Quellada lotion for "Total body lice and vermin." Quellada lotion was generally enough to kill all lice and vermin, but an additional treatment was required five days later to ensure that we'd kill all the eggs that may have been hiding safely just under the skin, and now would be emerging. This was definitely something that I would remind his nurse of, as nobody wants an infestation of lice, or vermin, or who knows what else on their body. The whole subject just makes you itchy, and in some cases a little paranoid that you might have been exposed, and now something is crawling on your skin. You may even have to stop reading and go check yourself out in the bathroom at some point during this story.

I told my co-worker Karl about the chart, and reminded him that his patient was due for another treatment. I then made my secondary round and actually entered Mr. Derby's room to speak to him about a couple of other things. I noticed he was very short, about 4'5", and I also noted he was practically bald, which was a plus, as lice would be easier to see or control. Mr. Derby, out of the blue, asked me, "Do you own any sheep?" to which I replied that I did not. "Do you like sheep?" he asked. "Not particularly," I said, "but I don't have anything against them, they're good for wool." He then said, "I really like sheep. They are so cute and soft, and they are very friendly." As he was talking, I had looked down at my to-do list and saw the notation about the Quellada lotion. Bang! It hit me, just like a shoe to the head, and I thought to myself, *Holy shit, this guy fucks sheep—that's how he got the total body lice and vermin, from hugging a sheep.* This was all in my head, they were just thoughts, and we can't always control every thought that goes through our heads, but he was still talking about petting the sheep, and had a rather sheepish grin on his face as he was describing it. *He screwed a sheep*, was the thought that popped back into my head.

When I left the room, I thought I had better warn Karl about what he may encounter when dealing with Mr. Derby. As I explained to him what Mr. Derby had said to me, and what popped into my head because of the sheepish grin on his face and the Quellada lotion, Karl snapped at me saying, "Come on, stop it—he has enough problems. Just because he looks a little weird and is a bit of a dwarf, you don't need to pick on him. Be nice." I said, "I'm telling you, I think that's where he got the total body lice and vermin," to which Karl responded with, "Fuck off, don't be an asshole." Karl was also a good friend and wasn't really mad at me but he did kind of give me the gears all weekend for what I had said. I assumed he would get over it; that's what friends do. Honestly, I was starting to feel a little bit like an ass for saying it. Next time, I thought, I would keep my mouth shut.

We had finished the long three-day weekend and decided to go out that Monday night for a drink. We were in our local honky-tonk, about eight of us at the table: Karl and I, and the rest non-medical workers. My fiancée and her friend were two of the eight. While Karl and I were listening to the conversation my fiancée and her friend were having with the rest of the group, one of the girls said something about barnyard animals, something about someone who was in the paper up on charges. My fiancée then said, "That sounds like that guy in middle school." Her friend said, "What guy?" And my fiancée replied, "You remember, we were at recess and the police came and had to pull him off of the sheep; he had it cornered against the fence and he was screwing it. We could all see it going on." Her friend then started nodding and began to laugh, as she said, "Right, I remember. Mr. Derby, the little midget, was putting it right to the sheep, and he screamed when they tried to pull him off!" At that point, Karl was taking a big sip of his beer, as was I, and we both spit it out—and I mean far. Karl actually hit two people on the other side of the table, and I was choking on mine. The people at the table weren't really mad about the beer being spit on them, but did get somewhat upset that we wouldn't share with them what we were actually laughing about. We let on it was an old joke between us, but I don't think they bought it. Karl put his hand on my shoulder and said, "Sorry, Jack, I will never doubt you again."

Some of you may think it was mean of me to share my thoughts with Karl, but I thought it was pertinent information at the time, and could be something we would need to know about the patient later if we encountered more problems in the future.

The reality is that maybe it was no laughing matter when we spit out our beer, but we are human, and all medical staff you have looking after you are human. Some may be near perfect, and some may be like Karl and me and find some things just too comical not to have a normal human reaction. But only those who are assholes go out and break confidentiality. Fortunately, they are few; most of us uphold the confidentiality rule even when it's killing us not to say something, just as we did that day.

As the years went on, I worked in many different hospitals and on a lot of psychiatric units, only to find that a shocking number of people engage in such behavior with animals. I had patients who'd had sex with cows, horses, dogs, sheep, young calves, and even one who'd done it with a tabby cat. There are a lot of sick and twisted people out there, and we nurses have to deal with each and every one of them. Ask yourself, if you had to cope with all of that, could you keep quiet about it? Remember that all of these people, regardless of their behavior, have family members in the community who don't need to be embarrassed, or be laughed at or ridiculed. Being loose-lipped can have severe consequences for both the patient and family members, and as a medical professional, it could cost you your job or liberties.

Hyperkalemia

When you have blood drawn, do you ever wonder what exactly we are looking to find? That little vial of blood is often only 3-5 cc or milliliters, about a teaspoon. Often, we are just doing a screen for various things like your hemoglobin, which is a blood cell that carries oxygen to the entire body, or your white blood cells, which help us figure out if your body is fighting an infection when these white cells will increase in number, or if you're at risk of not being able to fight an infection if the count is too low. There are many, many things that we could test for, and sometimes, one single lab value in that great big list of things can be extremely important if it is at the wrong level. Potassium is one of these, and it's what I will be talking about in this story.

One Sunday, I was working an afternoon shift. At about 4 p.m., I heard a Code Blue called, and that meant that a patient was likely under cardiac arrest or in some type of crisis. The code was in the ICU, so it was most likely an arrest, as the people in the ICU can handle most everything else, but extra staff are often required when someone's heart stops.

I was on the Code team that particular day, so I rushed off to the ICU, expecting to see some elderly patient or an overweight middle-aged man, such as myself, who had suffered heart failure.

I ran into the room, and that's when I saw a very tiny four-year-old boy lying limp on the mattress. One of my colleagues was already doing compressions on the boy.

When we run a Code in the hospital, the basic principles are similar to the way you learn CPR, as far as compressions, ventilations, etc. However, we have a lot of advantages while in an ICU, including access to a heart monitor and intravenous drugs that we push into the vein. We can intubate, which means putting a tube in the patient's throat to keep the airway open, then placing a mask over the patient's mouth that is attached to a bag to more easily control the amount of air going in. We can also draw blood from an artery in the lower abdomen near the pelvis to make sure that there is enough oxygen getting into the bloodstream. We do this to ensure our compressions are being performed adequately.

We always make use of all of these things, and I was especially thankful for them when our patient was a four-year-old boy. I had seen this child running down the hall on a previous shift. It was hard to believe such a small boy would have a bad heart. It was the first time I had coded a small child; it was a rare occurrence, in comparison to the elderly or obese. It did not fit the picture of what someone who was having a heart attack should look like.

I took over for the person doing compressions, as that was often the case, being one of the young and fit nurses at the time. Performing CPR is actually very hard on a person, and many adults have had a heart attack themselves while attempting CPR on another person. With a child it would be easier; I thought; at least physically. It was not; we only use one hand when performing CPR on people under eight years old, so as not to compress the ribs too far and cause harm. The child was about chest height, as the bed was elevated. To my surprise I tired very quickly and had to keep switching hands, which I was able to do to get the job done, but it took a lot out of me. It is horrible compressing anyone's ribs. We have to press far down enough to squeeze the heart and make it pump. Often, this fractures ribs, even when done perfectly. It was very hard seeing this little boy lying there with the life drained out of him. We tried compressions, gave medicine, shocked him with the paddles to restart the rhythm of his heart, drew blood from him to make sure we were doing our compressions correctly, which it appeared we were. I kept thinking that this boy should not be dying; he should be running around the hallway with his mother chasing after him, like I had seen the day before. I did not want to give up on this kid, and neither did the other five members of the Code team.

As we were desperately coding this young child, I happened to look up at the large window that formed a wall between the room and the hallway, and there I saw the boy's parents, looking in at what was happening to their son. I said, "Somebody has to get them out of there, take them away." We were all too busy to do so. I could only think that losing a child was bad enough, but seeing his last moments over and over again in their minds, if he died, would be even more traumatic.

Finally, we had to call the code as we had probably stayed at it too long as it was, and rigor was starting to set in, but we could not give up on this kid. I had been hoping that, like in the movies, just as everyone gave up the heart monitor would sound off with that distinctive beep. I was desperate to hear that sound. We waited and waited, and then I heard, "Time of death, 1734 (5:34 p.m.)." It was so painful, I almost yelled at the doctor, but he was right to call it; we had to.

As we were cleaning up and beginning to exit the room, I made it to the door first; I wanted to get as far away from that room as I could. As I looked up, I saw the child's father looking at me through teary eyes, with his hand outstretched. As I shook his hand he said, "Thank you for working so hard to try and save my little boy." Shock must have set in. Most parents, I would think, could not hold it together like that, at that moment.

When I got back to my floor, I had an hour and a half worth of work backed up, as nobody fills in for you when you are away. I was getting calls from everyone: patients calling with their call bells, other nurses asking questions, and the ward clerk asking me to do a bunch of tasks. One of the things I had to do was check a lab value on the computer, which froze up on me. I was feeling very hot, sweating, and became enraged. I stood up and kicked the monitor, which was sitting about four feet off the ground. When I struck it with my foot, it flew about seven feet in the air until the cord ran out. It then fell on the floor and smashed as I screamed a most distasteful word for all to hear—visitors and co-workers. It had been too much for me to handle. How could it not be? Who could walk away from such a sickening event and not be disturbed?

Later I would learn that the child had come to the hospital with some type of flu. He had been vomiting a lot and had many bouts of diarrhea, and it had been going on for several days. Sometimes, when we lose too many fluids and are not eating properly, our chemistry can be thrown off. Remember when I said that if even one lab value gets out of whack, it can be extremely dangerous? To prevent this from happening, sometimes the doctor will order an IV to be started, which has replacement electrolytes in it, potassium being one of them. In this case, it is important that we monitor a patient's K level (potassium level) to make sure we don't give them too much. Potassium is a very dangerous thing: too little or too much in your blood will stop your heart, usually starting with an arrhythmia.

Blood was drawn from the little boy, and what is referred to as a "panic level" was both called in to the unit and faxed over at about 6:00 a.m. Later that day, the child's heart stopped, as nobody went to the room immediately and discontinued the intravenous bag containing the potassium in it. In fact, an additional bag had been hung midday.

The first thing most people would think was that the nurse on duty was negligent, but this was not necessarily the case. It is routine in hospitals to have way too many patients to look after properly, as there would not be as much profit for the hospital if an extra nurse was assigned to each shift, which is exactly what should be done. Also, on this particular day, the hospital was so busy that the nurse may never have been informed of the emergency phone call, or have received the fax confirming the panic value of potassium at 6.2 mEq/L. Anything over 5.8 mEq/L is dangerous and should have been tended to. As much as I was upset by the boy's needless death, I knew it was not fair to blame the nurse on duty. It's extremely hard to keep on top of everything that needs doing when you are seriously understaffed, and this is the fault of the hospitals, which are, unfortunately, all about money.

I don't know what happened with the parents of the child, whether there was an investigation or a settlement or anything of that nature, but how could any amount of money ever make up for what they had gone through? It could not. The incident took a toll on me, as well. I still remember it as clear as day, that lifeless little body lying there, ashen in color, with rigor setting. This little boy wearing nothing but his Superman underwear. I had thought I'd put it behind me until several years later I had a four-year-old son myself, who also had a pair of Superman underwear. One day when I was doing his laundry, I was reminded of that tragic day, and I actually vomited into the washing machine. Every time *Superman* comes on TV, I get an uneasy feeling in the pit of my stomach, the memory of that little boy rushes into my head, and I feel like throwing up. My wife got upset with me on several occasions, as my son's Superman underwear kept going missing and I couldn't tell her why.

Love Thy Co-Worker

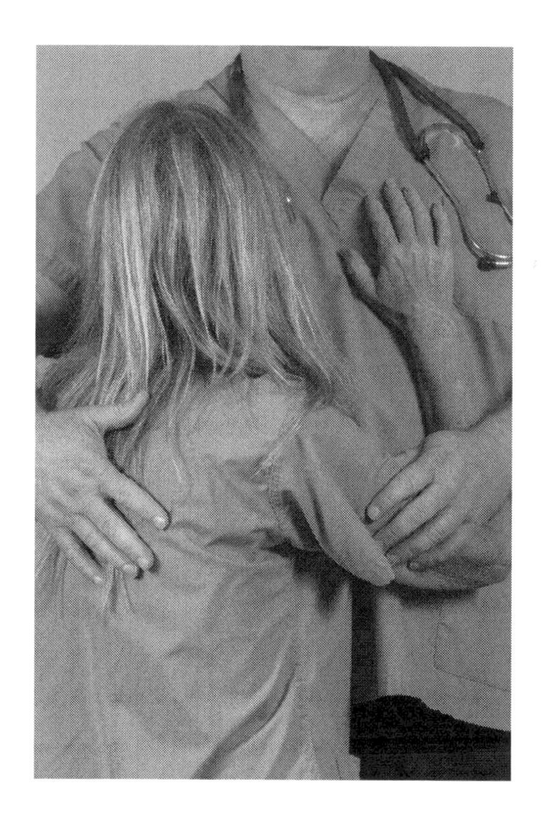

It is only natural that when you work with someone for a long time, day in and day out, you either begin to hate them, or you become really close—maybe even fall in love with them. The nursing field is no stranger to this phenomenon. In fact, at times, it is outright outrageous the amount of sex that is taking place between co-workers.

When I first started working at one particular hospital, I remember on more than one occasion, different nursing staff talking about the ghosts on the old, abandoned fifth floor. I've never believed in ghosts, but I realize that lots of people do, so when people started talking about the strange noises they heard from the fifth floor in the middle of the night—doors slamming, beds creaking, moaning and unexplained laughter—I just shook my head and kept my mouth shut.

I had to go up there one night to look for a wheelchair. I was informed that a lot of old equipment was stored on the now-vacant unit. One of the girls had asked me to go for her, as she heard noises and was afraid of the ghosts. As I walked down the hall, and turned into one of the old patient rooms, I heard squeaking and a moan, and as I rounded the corner, I saw one of my colleagues, a nurse whom staff jokingly referred to as "Bobby Bang 'Em Hard," riding one of the other nurses from another unit. I had caught them in the act. As it turned out, all of the noises that the staff on the unit below were hearing could be attributed to a randy group of co-workers—and there were many of them—who had basically set up a sex room and were partaking in doing each other's spouses. Well, not all of them were married, but many of them were.

It was none of my business, so I just exited the area and kept my mouth shut. Every time after that, when I heard the nurses talking about the haunted floor above them, I just smiled and thought, *I wonder if I could talk anyone into taking a lunch break up there with me?* Single women only, I mean. Alas, no such luck for me, but the place finally got dismantled when one of the nursing staff caught his wife up there with a co-worker, which led to a whole whack of problems for everybody involved.

One cold winter night, while working on a long-term psychiatric unit, my colleagues and I had managed to make it to midnight and all the patients were in bed. This meant that lights were out. Staff would visit for a while, then maybe go to the television rooms at either end of the floor to watch some shows to help stay awake. I was just thinking of going to the east end to watch some TV, when Mindy came into the office and said, "Well, Moe is down there with that dirty thing again, so if you want to watch any TV, you better go to the west end." I was fairly new and did not know all the characters on the unit yet. I listened for a while as the other three nurses bitched and complained about "that dirty whore" who "didn't deserve her husband" and looked like a "Collie dog." It went on like that for quite some time before one of them said, "Holy shit, you were right!" as she pointed to the surveillance monitor, which for the most part was dark, as the lights were turned out. We could see Moe's big white ass moving up and down as he humped Sherill, the woman the nursing staff had been deriding. The other nurses were pissed at what they saw on the monitors. About an hour later, Sherill came down the hall and into the nursing station. She said, "How's it going down here? It's quiet at the other end," as she opened the door to the bathroom at the back of the nursing station and went over to the sink. She then pulled out a bottle of mouthwash and began to gargle, with the door still open. One of the nurses yelled at her, "You goddamn pig, shut the door, you whore!" Well, after that things really began to heat up. All four women were yelling and fighting. I exited the room to the hallway, just as Moe was about to enter the room. I said, "You don't want to be in there," and we walked to the other end, to another office. I informed him about what the nursing staff were fighting about, and he said as he laughed, "I don't know why they're so upset with Sherill; I've had sex with the other two in there, here on the floor lots of times." He had no shame, and I guess neither did they.

At that same hospital, one of the doctors used to make rounds and made a lot of friends on various units. One friendly nurse—and I mean she was friendly with a lot of people—was caught on top of him one night in a break room by another nurse who went in to get her coat. Shocked by what she saw, she had said, "Oh, I'm sorry to bust in on you like that," and quickly exited the room. But afterwards she wondered why she had apologized. It was the break room, after all, and they shouldn't have been fooling around on their spouses. "This place is a zoo," she said to us, as she shook her head. "It's like we should just expect that as the norm around here, bunch of pigs! Doctor Shot-Spot should know better than that." This was a nickname he had picked up from another encounter weeks before that particular night.

Throughout my career, I encountered too many of these types of situations to list them all. People were caught bent over the control panel in the security room; at the time they were accidently leaning on the buttons that controlled the intercom on the unit, which made for interesting conversations with the patients the next morning at breakfast. Staff were caught in other people's offices going at it, in the backs of cars, in the employee parking lot, under camera surveillance, in the tunnels, stairwells, medication room, leaning over the medication cart, in the treatment room, utilizing the stirrups on the treatment table. There was so much sex between staff over the years, you just wouldn't believe—well, some wouldn't, anyway.

So, if you ever hear of there being ghosts or strange noises at your place of work, you never know what might really be going on. Just be careful whom you ask to go on break with you—they may have a reputation you're not yet aware of.

Little Big Man

My father would often use the term "Little Big Man" when talking about one of his enemies, or someone he despised, enemy or not. He explained it to us when we were kids that a "Little Big Man" is like that "little sawed-off prick over there," and pointed to a man at the local park whom he'd had several disagreements with in the past. "He's small but talks like a big man, and never shuts his fucking mouth. He thinks he knows everything and never stops talking over everyone else, like that little shit over there." The guy he was pointing at was about five feet tall, giving orders to a bunch of other volunteers at the time, while they were constructing a new soccer field for us kids. It was certainly not a *Webster's Dictionary*–style definition, but it always stuck with me.

I have run into a number of these types of people over the years, but none stood out as much as the Little Big Man I am going to talk about now.

Working in health care is hard. No matter where in the world you are, the job is just full of challenges and danger all the time. So, when you have to deal with a doctor such as our Little Big Man—our Dr. Basinger—it is even more of a challenge. He was the type of man who was pleasant when he wanted to be, and a prick in the very next breath—which was often foul-smelling. He did not have a good relationship with his toothbrush, as evidenced by his breath and his visibly dirty teeth. He was about 5'2" tall and about 45 years of age, with a thick French accent. He would often have the same mustard stain on his shirt two days in a row, and sometimes would have his dress shirt on inside out. How the hell does one even manage that? Think about it!

LBM would treat the staff on his unit like gold, bring them flowers during Nursing Week, donuts every Friday, and would often be heard praising the staff that worked on his unit. But if new people came onto the unit, or part-time nursing staff, he would blatantly ignore them. Even if the person was the nurse in charge for the day, he would say, "I don't want to talk to you, out of my way," and wave them aside with a sweeping arm motion. He would then go and talk French, in our English-speaking hospital, with one of his desired nursing staff who also was fluent in his mother tongue. When he would be on call, meaning covering the entire hospital for any medical emergencies, nursing staff who worked on other floors would be reluctant to call him, because he would usually say to them, "Why are you calling me? He's not my patient! Don't bother me, do your job, have his doctor see him in the morning." He knew damn well it was his responsibility to tend to the situation, but would avoid his responsibilities if the patient's primary doctor was somebody that he did not particularly like as a person. This was not the best way to operate a hospital and care for patients.

One Saturday evening as I started my shift, the charge nurse for the day asked me for some advice. She said, "Dr. Basinger told me to lock Mr. Roland in his cell and to leave him there for the weekend, and to only let him out for one hour a day, but he would not place him on a form." She was referring to a form that the doctor had to fill out, explaining why the patient was being locked up against their will, and, in turn, a patient advocate would come and speak to them, and inform them of their rights. It was all perfectly legal if you did the job properly and filled out the paperwork. But, Dr. Basinger, being the asshole that he was, decided that he did not want to do that extra work, so he wasn't going to do it. The system is set up this way to protect patients, or we could lock them up whenever we pleased without anyone knowing, especially if they were not on the ball or incompetent. This young nurse, Kathy, was almost in tears as she knew the law and the doctor was telling her to break it, something for which she could get in a lot of trouble. I told her she did a good job and had charted everything appropriately, and that I would look after it.

I called LBM, explained the situation, and told him that we needed him to sign the proper paperwork for everything to be legal—not that he really needed a reminder, but I was trying to tread softly as they say. His response was, "I told her, and now I am telling you, lock him up until Monday, I will reassess him then. Let him out one hour a day to the common areas and the yard, and then lock him back up." I explained to LBM that I couldn't legally do that, without the proper paperwork it was against the law. Every nurse knows these things. He then said, "You do what I say; I don't give a fuck what you think. You can whine and cry about it all you want, I do things my way—you can call the administrator if you want, I don't give a fuck." He then abruptly hung up on me.

I did call the administrator, who was actually a really nice guy, but like a lot of others, he was scared shitless of the doctor with Little Big Man syndrome.

I thoroughly explained the entire situation. He said, "Well, thank you, Jack, for bringing this to my attention. I will speak to Dr. Basinger, Monday," to which I said, "Wait a minute, this is Saturday evening. We can't wait until Monday—it's against the law." The administrator then said, "You're right. Oh, Dr. Basinger, what are you thinking?" He told me that he would call Dr. Basinger and get back to me. Two hours went by before I called the administrator again. Our pleasant and polite but gutless administrator said, "Well, I spoke to him and he said we could talk to him Monday about this and the best thing for everyone now, for safety, is to leave the patient locked up until Monday." I said, "That's not the point. The patient is dangerous and should be locked up, probably for a long time, but we have to do it legally." I was then told, "You did a good job, Jack. You've handled this well, but for now do as the doctor says." I knew if I let the guy out of the locked cell, he would most likely hurt someone, and I would lose my job for sure. Needless to say, the patient remained locked up for the weekend.

I was back the next Thursday, so I went to the administrator's office early into my shift and spoke with my boss. I said, "So how did your talk go with Dr. Basinger?" He said, "Well, I haven't had time to address it yet." Their offices were beside each other. It had been three days; there was ample time to do so, especially when a crime was being knowingly committed—and it was not the first time, to my mind, that this doctor had committed a crime. I checked in weekly with the administrator for about a month, but he still hadn't addressed it with the Little Big Man.

LBM's reign of terror would go on and on. There was another incident where a nursing manager stood up to him, as he was way out of line and not acting in accordance with the guidelines laid out by the American Medical Association. He managed to get her fired on a trumped-up bunch of lies that both he and another nursing manager, who was also a dud, had fabricated. The administrator had to fire her—or, at least, that's what he did.

She, the woman who was fired, was one of the best nurse managers I have ever seen. She would always do the right thing, sticking up for her staff and the patients. Nice gals finish last, I guess.

This guy got so many people fired—even the administrator who was kissing his ass got the axe eventually. Thankfully, Dr. Basinger pissed off so many people that he got himself fired in the end. I won't go into those details as many of them were not exactly known to the staff, but when he was being walked out of the building, many staff went out to the hallway and clapped.

It was amazing to experience how well the place ran after this very mean individual wasn't there anymore, putting our jobs in jeopardy, ridiculing and swearing at us, and belittling us all the time. If you have one of these Little Big Men in your life, be patient. Most often, they will eventually be the cause of their own downfall.

I'm Not Sure If I'm Gay

We hear the term "coming out" a lot, as in "he just came out." It's like a big announcement, like the person just realized they were gay and thought they should tell everybody. Well, a person does not just wake up one day, and out of the blue, realize, *hey, I'm gay.* In reality, a person has known this for some time. In other words, they have been attracted to the same sex for a while. It doesn't happen overnight, but, sometimes, a person may decide overnight that they will come out. More likely than not, however, they have been struggling with coming out for a long time. It is sad that they should have to struggle with this . . . What's to think about? Sadly, there's a lot, not the least of which is whether their family, friends and co-workers will be accepting of the fact. Then there is the bias and homophobia that is, unfortunately, ever-present in society. We have come a long way in the last couple of decades as far as acceptance goes, but we still have a long way to go.

One summer we had an 18-year-old boy admitted to our unit. I call him a boy, even though technically he was a man, but he sure did not seem to be up to the task. He was somewhat fragile, or weak in many ways, and acted very juvenile. He had a lot of maturing to do, but most of us do at 18, we just think we are men. Anyway, this kid had been arrested on an assault charge but also had a mental illness, and that was why he was with us, to receive an assessment to see whether or not he was criminally responsible and able to stand trial. After a couple of weeks, he seemed to settle into the unit, and for the most part, did what he was told, got along fairly well with staff and other residents, and didn't break any major rules, which is hard for these offenders.

One Monday morning when I reported to work, staff were saying that Saturday evening, he was caught having anal sex with another resident in the male dorm room. Since then, they had been watching him fairly closely, as he was very embarrassed and had been crying the majority of the weekend. He apparently had been heard yelling at staff, "I'm not gay! I'm not really gay!"

It had gotten to the point that some staff were worrying whether or not he was suicidal, so I was tasked with meeting with him and the on-duty doctor. We asked him about what had happened, and he admitted that he'd had anal sex with the other resident, and that he had thought about killing himself, but he had fathered a young child out on the street, and he couldn't decide if he should kill himself or not. The patient was very upset, crying profusely; it was very hard to get him to stop crying long enough to understand what he was trying to say to us. He said, "Why does it have to be that big a deal? All the guys have been making fun of me all weekend and won't let it go." The doctor then asked who was making fun of him, and the patient said, "Larry and Bill."

The doctor said, "Who? They must be Dr. Kenny's patients. Anyway, it doesn't matter. You need to ignore them, stay away from them, and let staff know if you have a problem with them in the future." The problem with that was that Larry and Bill were both staff from the night shift—that's right, staff—and they were teasing this poor kid to the breaking point. I had known them to act out of line before, but usually they were pretty good with patients. Other times, though, they could be genuine assholes. The patient started blubbering again, saying, "I'm not sure if I'm gay or not. I don't think I am . . . no, I don't think I am, not really." The doctor didn't seem to have anything else to add, so I said, "Listen, Kyle, I'm going to tell you something. If you ever look down and see that you have an erection, and you're inside another man, you're gay. You don't accidently trip and fall and become hard while falling, and end up inside another man, so you're gay, and, really, who gives a fuck? I don't, and neither do the people who are teasing you; they just know that it bothers you. Most people don't give a shit if you're gay or not. Fuck whoever you want if it feels good and they're a consenting adult. Fuck them and enjoy it, just be more discreet about it in the future." Both Kyle, our distraught patient, and the on-duty doctor just stared at me, apparently in disbelief. Then, after a long, pregnant pause, the doctor joined in and said, "Yes, fuck whoever you want. We don't care and neither should you."

A look of extreme relief came over Kyle's face and he said, "Thanks, guys. Thanks for talking with me." He then left, and the elderly doctor just stared at me for a moment and then said, "Brilliant, that was fucking brilliant. Good job, Jack, well done."

You have to understand, these patients are usually picked on. Some of them—or most of them—are more receptive if you just give it to them straight; don't beat around the bush, talk in a manner they will understand. Talking to most patients in a general hospital setting like that will get you fired in a hurry, but when you are good at assessing a patient—and I was—it is often more effective to speak to them in their language; they will respect you if you have been kind to them and treated them well in the past. It's about building a level a trust.

This turned out to be the best treatment that this young man could get: an authority figure giving him permission to be who he was, without shame. Kyle ended up staying with us a long time, and I ended up disciplining him for many things over the course of his stay, but even then he came to his last treatment conference and repeated what I said to him that day to the group, and then said, "Thanks, Jack. If you wouldn't have been so nice to me and talked to me the way you did, no bullshit, like you did with me, I think I would have done something stupid that day, like kill myself. I owe you a lot."

Some of the female nurses were shocked that I'd said what I did to him, but they understood the logic behind it. Staff put themselves on the line a lot, like I did that day. If the wrong person heard me saying those things, things could have gone very wrong for me. But this kid needed help, and that was exactly the kind of help he needed to come to terms with himself. None of what I said was taken in a derogatory way by the patient, and it was the only way, in the moment, that I knew to help him. Far too many young kids have killed themselves because they were terribly distraught over this very same thing. Kyle's name did not need to be added to that list.

Mama

When you're a nurse on a long-term-care psychiatric ward, staff become very familiar with their patients and vice versa. It is inevitable that some of them grow on you, and some of them tend to take a shine to particular staff, as well. Often, we get to know our patients better than many of our own family members. It makes perfect sense. You work with them for 12 hours a day; that's 2,050 hours a year. And you may see your aunts, uncles, siblings, and sometimes even your parents, for a mere three hours per holiday, five days out of the year. The math is pretty easy.

We had one elderly lady, only 63 years of age, but she'd lived a hard life and looked 80 years old if she looked a day. She would often be seen walking about the unit, placing a blanket over either a staff member or fellow patient who had fallen asleep in front of the television. She liked to stand with nursing staff monitoring the meals. She would always greet you with a big smile in the morning, when she came down to breakfast. She could often be heard singing, but rarely made it through a chorus before she would start coughing excessively. She had been a terrible smoker all her life and now had COPD (chronic obstructive pulmonary disease). Basically, her lungs were shot, and it was always a struggle to keep cigarettes away from her, as she was so pleasant with other patients and could often talk them into giving her one. Psychiatric patients smoke more than any other population.

Now let me get back to Mama's singing. She started singing to me one day and grabbed ahold of my arm when I was trying to dispense my medications. She began singing, "You are my sunshine, my only sunshine." You've probably heard the rest. She was obviously not going to stop, so I let her finish the song, holding on to my elbow, and as she finished the song, she leaned in and looked straight into my eyes, with a big smile on her face as she ended the song. She then coughed and said, "May I have a cigarette, Monsieur?" I said, "No, I'm sorry, Mama, I don't have any, and your doctor has said you are not to be given any cigarettes." This sweet old lady, who looked a lot like my grandmother and had just serenaded me, suddenly yelled, "Fuck you, you cocksucker! I'll smash your fucking face in!" and began punching me.

Well, I must say that was a surprise to me. The other nurses just laughed and said, "It's your turn today, better you than us." But with Mama's dementia, and having mental illness on top of that her whole adult life, it was not hard to see why she behaved the way she did. A half hour later, she was asking if I needed any milk or eggs and offering to go buy them for me at the store. Then, before she could make her way to the locked door, she became side-tracked by another patient and began singing to her.

As angry as this elderly woman was, and as dangerous as she could be, we were her family. She was our patient whom we provided care for over the course of many years, and when she finally succumbed to a bad bout of pneumonia/heart failure, we all missed her. The other patients on the unit even held a bereavement ceremony, as they missed her, too. She was their family, as well. Even the troublesome patients have their good points. After all, nobody chooses to be mentally ill. This is often the case in long-term-care settings. When you start school, you're told not to become emotionally connected to your patients, but in cases like this, it is hard not to get used to someone being around for so many years, and then, when they pass away, feel the void. We are, after all, human.

It's a Timex!!!

Most of us have busy schedules and often feel as though we just don't have enough time to finish everything we need to get done. Often, we can be found sneaking peeks at our watches to see where we're at, in regards to our schedule—if we are going to make it, or if we are falling behind and need to pick up the pace. For some of us, even if we are not in a hurry, keeping track of time elapsed is nearly impossible, especially if we have any type of cognitive delay or mental illness that may affect our ability to focus or concentrate on the most basic of tasks.

On a lot of psychiatric units, patients are locked on the unit and not able to leave by themselves until they are more stable. Certain patients never progress as well as we would like them to, but eventually, if they are not violent, we have to give them a chance to leave the building on their own. The passes are brief at first, and as time goes on, they graduate from one-hour intervals, to two hours, then three. Usually they have to report back before the time is up or they risk losing their privileges. It is not so much a punishment (though it must feel like it to the patients) as a safety protocol. Patients have to prove themselves for a while before they are able to progress, as they are not always stable and may wander off and get into trouble.

I remember one particular patient we had who had lived at the facility for about 15 years and was 33 years of age. So, he had been with us basically his whole adult life. He was very ill, as he suffered from schizophrenia. Schizophrenia is an illness that causes a person to have one episode after another of psychosis, hallucinations, delusions, lack of motivation, and often can't be controlled well enough with medication for a person to lead a normal life. Mario, my young Italian friend, was one of the most severely affected individuals with whom I have ever worked.

When at his best, Mario could go out on his own for extended periods of time without getting into too much trouble, but at other times, he could not function well enough to do so and was always returning late, as he could not think clearly enough to keep track of time. He would return to the unit 15 or 20 minutes late, which meant he would lose his privileges for 48 hours. We would give them back to him, and he, in turn, would go out on the grounds or to the patient canteen for his hour, but would again return late only to lose his privileges. We even made sure his watch was working; we checked the time when he left and compared it to when he got back. The watch was not the issue; his brain was. He just could not function well enough to keep track of time.

One day he came back 35 minutes late, and we talked to him about this. One of the nurses said, "Mario, no wonder you're late . . . you didn't even take your watch. Did you leave it in your room or sell it at the canteen for a cigarette?" Mario's response was "The watch makes me late; it's evil. It's the watch that's making me late. It controls me, don't need it anymore, it's evil." The nurse said, "The watch can't make you late but if you forget to look at it, you will be late. You have to focus better or set an alarm." Regardless, he lost his privileges again.

After two more days had passed, we expected Mario would go out on his privileges again, but he didn't show up for the lineup of patients who would be going out that morning, and again in the afternoon he failed to show up. He had also missed both breakfast and lunch, which in itself was not uncommon on a schizophrenia unit. People who suffer from this affliction often have a hard time mustering the energy to get out of bed in the morning, and the medication they take at night is very sedating and can cause a hangover effect the next morning.

Anyway, I approached Mario, who was lying on his bed. He said he didn't feel well; he had a stomachache. Naturally, I checked him out, as a lot of people on this type of unit can become extremely constipated due to a combination of both medication and inactivity. He did not seem constipated when I felt his abdomen, but he did have pain when I depressed my hand on the lower right portion of his abdomen. This was often a sign of an appendix that may be inflamed, but the pain was felt when I pushed down. Usually with an inflamed appendix, the pain increases when you remove your hand. Also, he did not have a temperature, which often accompanies an appendix problem, depending on how far along it is. I had his doctor assess him, to no end, but he did have us transport him to the general hospital to do an X-ray.

Later that afternoon we received a phone call asking for Dr. Hernandez, the doctor who had sent Mario for the X-ray. The ward clerk handed the phone to the doctor, and I heard: "Hello? . . . What? . . . What do you mean? . . . What, on the X-Ray? . . . Are you sure? . . . Really, are you pulling my leg? Oh, oh for fuck sakes, that's awful, fuck! . . . Okay, yes . . . Okay, we will take him right back . . . Okay, I will call you later." Dr. Hernandez hung up the phone, turned toward us, and said, "Mario swallowed his fucking watch!!!" He had indeed swallowed his watch—I saw the X-ray myself—and it had gotten hung up on his caecum, which is at about the same location as the appendix.

Mario required surgery to remove the watch and was in the hospital for a couple of days, but made it through okay. He had a small incision, with eight staples that I removed a week later, as ordered. About ten days later, we were talking to Mario about the watch and why he swallowed it. He said, "It was always making me late to get back to the ward and causing me to lose privileges, so I ate it." In his delusion, it was the fault of the watch that he was losing privileges, so he ate it, problem solved; now the watch couldn't make him late anymore. You would think that his statement would have surprised us, but it didn't; we'd had patients eat or swallow batteries, quarters, Lego, dice, stones, a spoon, asphalt, dinky cars, you name it. If they can get it down, a patient somewhere has probably swallowed it. It's sad, but it happens a lot.

Dr. Hernandez tried to cheer Mario up and said, "Well, just try your best to be on time. Do you need to buy a new watch?" Mario answered, "No, the doctor at the hospital gave it back to me," and he held up his wrist and was wearing the same Timex that he had swallowed.

Later, when Mario had left, I said to Dr. Hernandez, "We should get him to sign a release and send it to the Timex company. He can probably sell that story: 'Not only does it take a licking, but you can swallow it, too, and it keeps on ticking!'" Dr. Hernandez agreed, "Yes, yes, we should do that. Let's do it, get him to sign the release." I then said, "Doc, I was kidding, he's not competent, remember?" to which Dr. Hernandez replied, "Oh, fuck yes, what was I thinking? No, no, we should not do that, Jack, definitely not."

Ever since that day, whenever Mario was late, the first thing staff did was check to see if he was wearing his watch.

Red-Faced Student

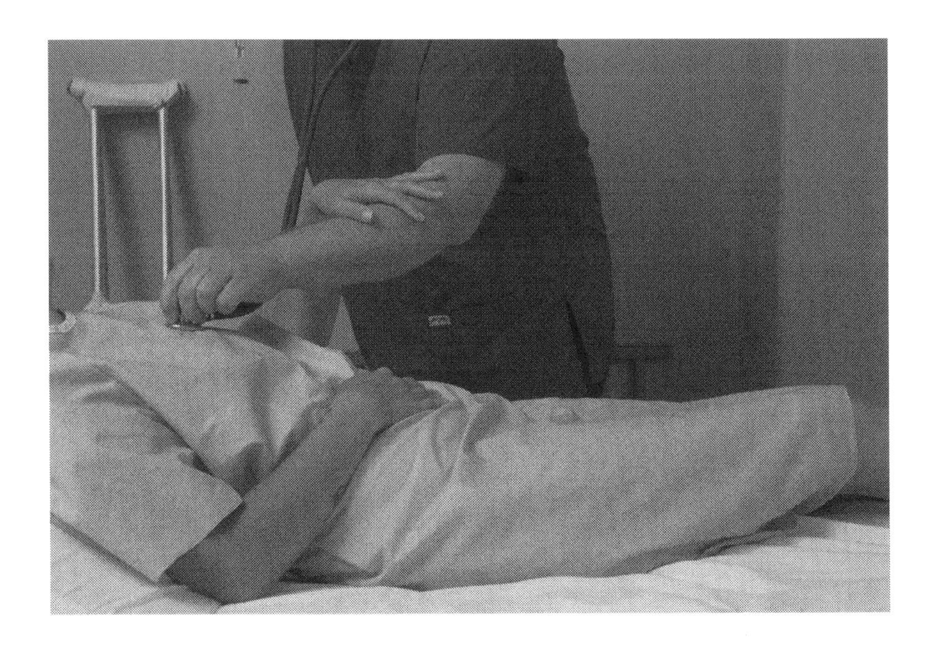

I don't believe that people really understand how embarrassed nurses or most health care workers, for that matter, can get, at times. We all are somewhat embarrassed to disrobe and don a paper gown when we go to a doctor's office for a check-up, or are admitted to the hospital and a nurse asks us to pull down our pants so they can jab a big needle into our butt. Everyone can relate to that, but have you ever considered how the nurse feels? Maybe the nurse is equally embarrassed, shy, disgusted or afraid. There are an infinite number of emotions that might arise in these types of scenarios—emotions on the part of both the patient and the nurse.

When I was 20 years old, I was finished the academic portion of school/my courses. I was doing a six-month placement on a medical-surgical unit, where I was generally paired up with a full-time registered nurse. This was a definite way to polish your skills, or in most cases learn new ones, as school can never fully prepare anyone to become a nurse; we have to learn on the job while caring for patients—real people with real problems—and we do that under the guidance of an experienced RN, who has been there a while. Gradually, we start to do more procedures on our own. It's the only way to build confidence and become a real nurse.

One day near the end of my training placement, my regular preceptor was not there, and one of the other nurses was watching over me. Most procedures were familiar enough to me that I could do them on my own by that point. Any new procedures, or ones that I had not yet had a chance to take part in, were assigned to me. It's never possible to experience every type of situation while you're a student. You would have to be a student for 40-plus years. To that end, the experienced nurses knew that they should give me and the other students the opportunity to assist with every new procedure that presented itself.

One afternoon, I heard the other nurses arguing about me. I heard one nurse say, "That's not fair to him. She's too young; he'll be embarrassed." The other nurse, a large buxom woman, disagreed with the other staff. The other students had tagged her with the nickname, "Nurse Ratched," from the popular 1970s movie, *One Flew Over the Cuckoo's Nest*. Nurse Ratched went on to say, "No, she isn't too young and he is going to be a full-fledged nurse in a couple of weeks. He will be on his own and needs to be prepared to do this, and he is going to, and I don't want to hear any more about it." What Nurse Ratched said, or wanted, usually happened. I think I would be more afraid of her than her namesake from the movie.

They then proceeded to tell me that the patient was a young woman who was 26 years old and was post-operative, or had had surgery several days before, and she had not yet had a bowel movement despite being given a variety of laxatives. They went on to inform me that her doctor had given us an order to do a rectal exam to see if she was impacted with stool. We sometimes even had to do digital manipulation of the stool, to get things started. It was at that point that Nurse Ratched informed me that I would have to go in, explain the procedure to the patient, and, if she allowed me, I was to do a digital check. What that means is, I was to insert my index finger up the patient's anus and into the rectum to feel for hardened stool/poop.

I did not want to do this, but Nurse Ratched was correct. In a couple of weeks I would no longer be a student—time to grow up, and fast. I entered the room and proceeded to explain both the doctor's orders and the rationale, and how I would be doing the procedure. To my surprise, the patient said, "Okay, that's perfectly fine with me," and began to turn over onto her belly. I had fully expected—and hoped— that she would refuse my request and demand a female nurse. No such luck.

Now I actually had to perform this rectal exam on this young woman only six years older than myself. I, as always, was trying my best to be very professional; I closed the curtain to ensure her privacy. It was not the type of procedure anyone would want others to witness by accident. I then asked the patient to pull up her gown to expose her behind. I put some K-Y jelly on my gloved finger and then gently put my other hand on her buttock to separate her cheeks and make room to insert my finger as far as possible to more accurately assess the situation related to fecal impaction. As I began the procedure, I inserted my index finger about halfway—slowly, so as not to harm the patient, or cause pain. She suddenly moaned a little, and reached back and grabbed my other hand that was holding her buttock. I asked if she was in pain. She said no, keep going, and then she started moaning and rubbing my other hand— and her moans weren't the painful sort at all. I believe she was enjoying the procedure. She was moaning rather loudly by the time I could extract my finger and said, "Please, don't stop." When she turned around, she had an obvious smile of delight on her face. I didn't know what to do, other than get the hell out of that room as soon as I could. It was very embarrassing, as well as worrisome. The last thing any young male nurse wants is for someone to think they are being inappropriate with a patient; it is a career-ender, and one could land in jail, depending on what accusations might be made by the patient.

I was completely red-faced by this point; I knew it as I could feel the rush of blood to my face and head. I quickly opened the curtain to make a quick exit, only to find her rather imposing, muscular husband standing just beyond the curtain with his arms folded, as he gave me the most frightening look.

Just beyond him was Nurse Ratched. I quickly explained to her everything that had happened. Fearing the worst—that she would not believe me and things would go very badly for me—was very much on my mind. She stared at me for what was probably a couple of seconds, but seemed like ten minutes, and then shook her head and said, "That bitch, what the hell is wrong with her?" She then patted me on the shoulder and said, "I'll take care of her; you go do your charting." Nurse Ratched then entered the patient's room and I could hear her scolding the patient. The relief I felt at that point I am not even able to describe. She believed me, as she had been watching me closely for months and had formed her opinion about me. I was trustworthy in her eyes. All this time I had been trying to avoid her, as she was often grumpy, issued a lot of orders, and was very bossy most of the time. It turned out that her bark was definitely worse that her bite. Later I would learn that most people really loved working with her; she demanded respect and gave it when it really counted.

This is just one of the many experiences that I have had that caused worry or embarrassment for me. Keep that in mind, please: we nurses are just people. Often people think, "You're a nurse; you're used to it," but we still have feelings. What that patient did to me, probably just to upset her husband, was wrong and could have had very bad consequences for me.

If you have any friends who are nurses, I bet they have a dozen similar stories.

Sexually Transmitted Diseases

Not for me, that's what everyone thinks—but if you're having sex, you're rolling the dice. Ah, but if you're married, you're safe! Nope—still rolling the dice in some marriages. It seems like the worst thing that could happen when you're the one who has one of these infections. But really, it's just a bacteria, or virus; it shouldn't have to come with such a stigma, yet it does. At any rate, it's usually not the end of the world, and most STDs can be treated very easily nowadays.

I remember early in my career, I was giving a patient a needle for pain management. He had recently broken his leg and required surgery. After I had administered the needle, he said, "The doctor said my lab work should be back today, can you check for me?" So, about half an hour later, I entered his room and was about to review his lab results.

As I started to talk to him, the en suite bathroom door opened, and his wife walked out. I stopped and said, "I'll review this later when I have more time, and I'll let you enjoy your visit for now." He said, "No, no, it's okay. She's my wife, you can say whatever in front of her, no big secrets between us," and he smiled. I said, "Really, I have other things to attend to. I'll be back shortly."

I came back to answer the call bell about an hour later. His wife was still there. He asked me point-blank, "Can you tell me if there is anything wrong with my blood work, the urine test, or that swab thing they did? I'd like to find out before my wife leaves, so she won't worry or anything." He was very insistent, so I told him everything was okay with the exception of an infection in his urinary tract, but we could treat that with antibiotics. "Really, are you sure?" he asked. "I feel fine down there—what kind of infection?" Then his wife piped up and said, "How could he get a bladder infection? Women usually get those." At this point, I had no choice, so I just put it out there. "Well, women and men can get infected with this. You have chlamydia." He sat still for a few seconds, then said, "No, that can't be right. I haven't had sex with anyone except my wife in 22 years." He then turned his gaze away from me and over to his wife, who had gone completely red-faced. She tried to divert her gaze to the floor, like that would help; it did not. The man looked very angry as he turned toward her and said, "You got to be fucking kidding me." She then broke into tears and quickly left the room.

Another time I was with the doctor when a man came in for elective surgery. He also had some drainage and redness in his eye. The doctor was making small talk with him and asked, "Did you ever get married?" Apparently, he knew the guy from high school. The patient said, "No, still playing the field; there's lots of me to go around." He said this in a joking manner. I did a swab at that time. A couple of days later, I was making rounds with the doctor and he had to inform the man that he did, in fact, have an infection in his eye, and it was due to gonorrhea. The patient said, "Gonorrhea? How could I get that in my eye? You get that from sex, so how did it get into my eye?" The doctor appeared very serious as he looked straight at the patient, and then, to my surprise, he broke out in song: "Looking for love in all the wrong places . . ." Both he and I, and eventually the patient, began to laugh. Johnny Lee was the name of the singer who sang that country song, and most people are familiar with it, but I had never heard it sung to a patient by a doctor to inform him he had an STD. It was actually hilarious.

In case anyone is confused, if a man was touching a woman's genitals, and she had gonorrhea, and then he were to wipe his eye, it would become infected; we refer to this as cross-contamination. Again, easy to cure, but not everything is.

A few years ago, on a medium-secure wing of a prison, a patient came into the clinic and said, "I have a little problem." I said, "Well, what is it? Maybe we can help." He said, "A few years ago, I got herpes on my penis from my boyfriend at the time and I think it's back." He then showed me his penis, which was plastered with erupting herpes all over the head and shaft. He was definitely experiencing some discomfort. I said, "No problem, I'll get some medicine ordered, and we'll help put out the fire." Herpes is a virus, so, we can't cure it, but we do have an antiviral cream that helps the process along and shortens the amount of time that the current vesicles will last. It works quite well, but still, you're going to feel it for a few days. I asked him if he needed any health instruction related to the affliction, and reminded him that he was very likely to spread it if he had intimate contact with anyone. He told me, "Don't worry, I know all about it. I've had this for a few years."

About ten days later, we had another patient on the same wing come to the clinic. He said, "I think I have something wrong with my anus; it's really sore. I thought it was hemorrhoids at first, but I'm worried now." One look at his anus and buttocks area made it pretty clear. I said, "Take, a look, Doc." Our clinic doctor asked the patient, "Have, you ever had herpes before?" The patient said slowly, "Ah, no . . ." "Well, you do now," the doctor informed him. The patient lowered his head and said, "That fucker." I said, "That's one way you can get it, yes—but it can also be transmitted through oral sex," and I went on to give him the rest of the health talk.

Still on the same wing and doing the doctor's clinic, I had yet another patient come and say, "I have these cold sores which really hurt, and I also have a bunch of sores on my ass and pecker, and I've never had these types of sores anywhere before now." It was herpes, Patient #3 to be diagnosed on that same unit. Herpes can take a few days to show up after contact with an individual who has a flare-up, and it can be spread even before the sores appear on the already-infected individual. So, you can't just look at someone's genitalia and do a visual inspection, and think, "No herpes there—we're good to go."

Oh, and FYI, there are two types of herpes: genital herpes and herpes simplex. People used to say the ones on your lips were herpes simplex—you can get that from kissing. I think it makes everyone feel better to be able to say, "I got it from kissing a girl," which they may have, but in reality, the only way to know the difference between genital herpes and herpes simplex is to view the virus under a microscope. So, you don't really know which one you have on your lips or your genitals without a test. They both cause the same pain and embarrassment, and they are with you for life. And to be really clear on this, A COLD SORE IS REALLY HERPES. So, don't go around kissing your kids when you have a cold sore.

Another thing that can be transmitted when we get friendly in the bedroom is crabs, or pubic lice. These parasites attach themselves to the pubic hair, and they hold on pretty tight. They dig into the skin, both for food and to lay their eggs. It's not a nice thought, but pubic lice doesn't cause a health risk—just a pain in the ass and pubic area. You usually don't have to wonder for very long if you have them; they will let you know as they are very itchy and you will find yourself scratching your crotch a lot.

On a psychiatric unit, a patient who suffered from chronic schizophrenia had picked up pubic lice, and the doctor had ordered a medicine that he was to use, but he had been refusing, for two days, to take a bath or wash with the medicine. He was a very large man, about 6'6" tall, and about 260 lbs. He was also one of the most ill patients we had ever had, and did not respond well to medications at all.

My task was to somehow talk him into taking a shower and applying the medicine to himself. The next step, if I failed to persuade him, was to call a bunch of men to the unit, and we would shower him and apply the lotion against his wishes. This was not a prospect I, or any other staff member, was looking forward to. It usually took about ten of us to seclude him when it was required. We had done this countless times over the years with this patient, and often somebody would get injured.

My first attempt was a failure. He told me, "Leave me alone or you're gonna fucking get this!" and held up his fist. I was not surprised at this, and actually expected as much. I waited about an hour, and then thought I would try again.

What you have to remember is that some of these people had lived in this institution for 40 years; it was their home. Many of them were very bored, and to put it simply, they smoked a lot and screwed a lot, often not with the same partner—it could be many. It's human nature. That being said, I still had to figure out how to talk this man into washing off his pubic lice, to eradicate them, so that the entire hospital did not have an outbreak. I decided to take a more friendly approach. I motioned for him to follow me, and when he did, I led him to a quiet area and placed my index finger in front of my lips—a common sign we use to indicate that we want the other person to stay quiet. I then whispered in his ear, "Hey, Sam, I'm worried about you. I know what that girl gave you, and I want to help. I have this shampoo, and I'm afraid if you don't get rid of those crotch crickets, you'll never get laid here again. Once the word gets out that you have crabs, nobody will want to fuck you." He looked hard at me, with a grimace on his face, and I thought for a minute I made the wrong call and he might attack me. He then said, "Hey, you're right. Thanks pal. How do I put it on?"

Problem solved. He complied; my unconventional approach had worked. Before you judge me for being unprofessional and vulgar, remember, this guy was used to talking like that, and coming off as an authority figure would not work. I talked to him like one of his friends would, and I had worked with him for years and knew him well. I felt this was a better approach than a big fight to get him into the shower, and the strong possibility that either the patient or staff would be injured again. People who are nurses, and especially seasoned ones, already know this. The goal is always to help your patient in the most humane fashion. Which I believe I did.

Most of the above stories I've attempted to tell in a comical manner, but sometimes the diseases we spread are just too serious to make light of. About 30 years ago, I was working alongside a colleague and friend. She was 24 years old, a single mother, and a blonde beauty. She was a very nice person, too. At the beginning of an afternoon shift, she came out of the adjacent room that I was about to enter, and she was crying and holding her finger. She had stuck herself with a dirty needle. A dirty needle refers to one that has already been in a patient. She was attempting to milk the blood out of her finger and quickly becoming hysterical—for good reason, as the needle belonged to an AIDS patient. She had to leave work and go to the emergency room. She then had to take a few days off before she could return.

Back then, if my old brain can remember correctly, I think you had to wait at least six months to find out whether you had contracted HIV (human immunodeficiency virus), which causes AIDS. Even with a needle stick, a person has a chance that they won't contract the virus—thank God—or most of us hospital staff would not be living. Most medical personnel have at least one incident of exposure to something that is potentially deadly during their career. My friend was back at work and doing fine, until a few months later, she heard what nobody ever wants to hear: she had contracted HIV. At that time, we did not have the phenomenal medications that we have now to treat HIV, and sadly, the ones we had back then weren't enough to save my friend; she didn't make it past 30. This type of accidental exposure has claimed the lives of many hospital staff over the years. It is very, very sad indeed.

Wow, She's Agile

When we are young, we do what we like, when we like, as far as physical movement. If a kid takes a notion to run, or jump high, or off of an elevated perch, they just do it. When we age, we all realize that we are not as pliable as we once were, and it can often take a lot of effort and dedication in the gym to keep ourselves fit enough to play sports, jog, skate, or whatever it is you enjoy doing.

I once had an elderly patient, 79 years of age, who required an IV to be hooked up to receive some vital medicine. So, I started the IV and securely taped it down on her arm, and left the room. About 30 minutes later, one of the nurse techs came and informed me, "Your patient in Room 2 accidently pulled out her IV." So, I started it again, and taped it more securely, counseling the woman on positioning and telling her to call for help if she needed to use the toilet, etc. A short while later as I was doing my rounds, I discovered that she had pulled out the IV again.

Something was wrong, and I was very suspicious that she just did not want the IV in her, and most likely was pulling it out on purpose. I restarted it again, counseled her again, and said I would be back to check on her soon. She said, “I will take good care of it,” and I left the room but remained just out of sight of the patient. I waited about 30 seconds before poking my head around the corner, where I saw her pulling at the tape that I had just placed on her arm. Before I could get to her, she had yanked out the IV again.

Clearly, she was not going to let us give her the medicine via IV. I called her doctor, who at that time gave an order to restrain the patient’s wrists while the IV was in, and she would reassess her in the morning. It is never something that we want to do—restrain people against their will. It’s not nice for them at all, and they often become combative, angry and very hard to deal with. She was no exception. She fought us at first, when we attempted to secure her arms with the restraints, but eventually we managed to restrain her without hurting her, which is always tricky. I waited around and talked with my very angry patient, who would periodically shake her head in disgust and mutter, “You prick.”

After about 30 minutes, the nurse tech hollered down the hall, “She’s at it again!” I quickly went to the room in time to stop her, as she was almost out of the restraints. I secured the restraints, slightly tighter this time. I figured we were all good now, so I left her room. To my surprise, the nurse tech soon hollered, “Come back here, now!” as she waved me over and ran ahead of me into the room. She reported to me how she saw Mrs. Taylor pulling the IV out of her arm. She explained how the patient, who had her wrist tied to the bedrail beside her waist, had leaned forward and pulled the IV out with her teeth.

After talking to her doctor again, I received orders to give Mrs. Taylor a sedative, and proceed with the IV and restraints one hour after she took the sedative. The sedative worked great. Mrs. Taylor was very cooperative, and even smiled as we were tucking her in and fixing her pillows.

About a half hour later, I was entering Mrs. Taylor's room, just in time to witness her pulling out the IV that was in her left arm with her right foot. She had her toes wrapped around that IV line as well as most people could have done with their fingers. As she pulled the IV out, she looked up and said, "How do you like that, you fucker?" You don't often hear that kind of language coming from a 79-year-old woman in the South. I must admit, she was beginning to annoy me.

When you take a nursing job, you never expect to see something like this. Mrs. Taylor (Houdini?), at 79, was able to do something—pulling out her IV with her foot—that most 20-year-olds would have difficulty with. The elderly have surprised me on more than one occasion with the physical feats they are capable of, especially when they are not in their right mind, be it due to dementia, psychosis, high fever, or just plain fear.

Never underestimate the elderly: they may just be more fit than you think, and more agile.

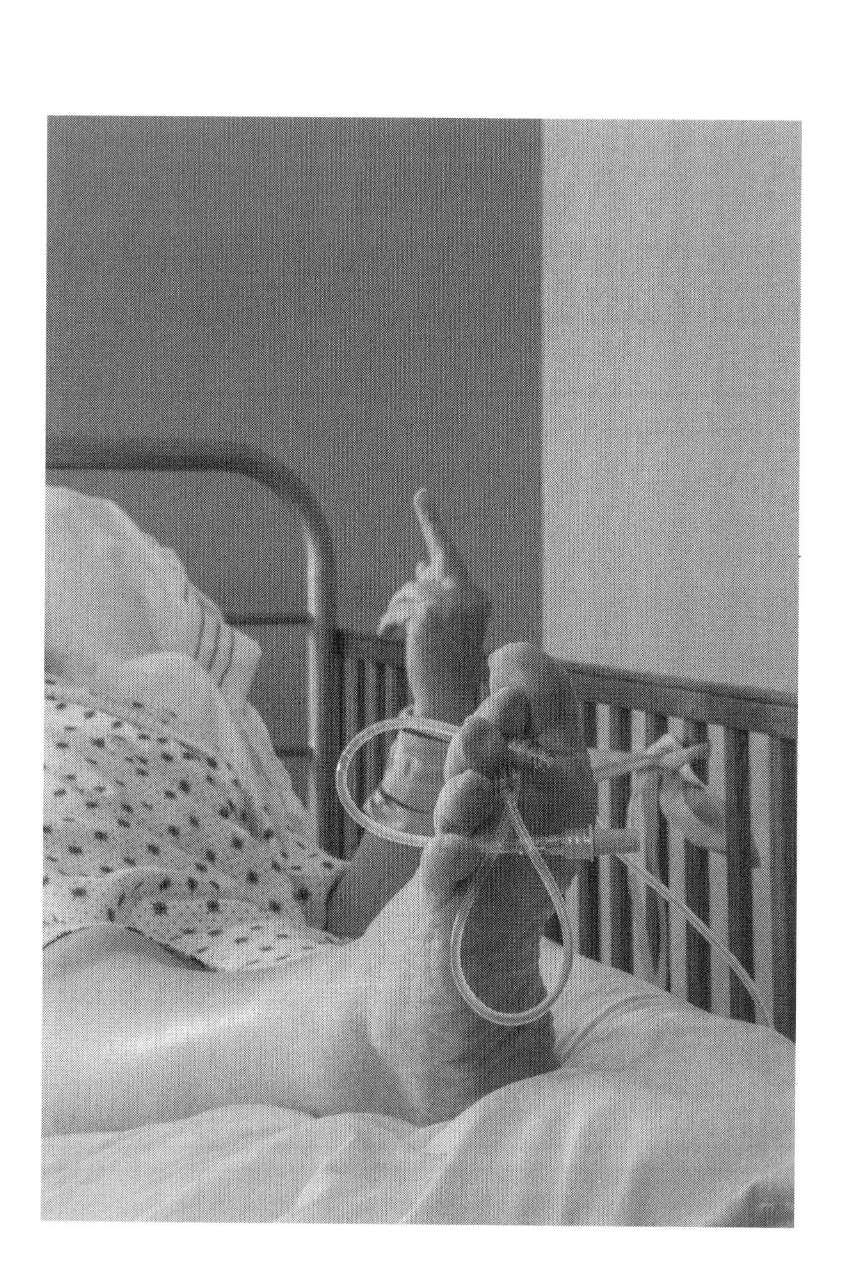

You're Not Pregnant

Being pregnant is a big event, whether it's your first time or tenth time. It is also a big deal when the pregnancy is unplanned, or unwanted. Can you imagine being a woman who is pregnant, and nobody will believe that you are? It would be infuriating and distressing to any woman to be faced with this.

We had a patient come into the acute psychiatric unit one time who claimed she was pregnant. She was 43 years old, white, unkempt, overweight, and looked as though she had been living on the street, as she most likely was. This woman was single, with no children, but in her chart there was a notation that she'd had an abortion several years before. She had also been hit with a snowplow and thrown about 20 feet only to be hit by a taxi. Needless to say, she had been through a lot. She also suffered from schizophrenia, which was her primary diagnosis, and the one that usually caused her the most grief.

It was responsible for her many trips to the psychiatric hospital. I had overheard her earlier, at breakfast, telling another patient, "I have to drink the milk; I'm pregnant." I had also been told in report that she was obsessed with being pregnant, but was not, as a pregnancy test had been performed on her and she was definitely not pregnant.

Sarah had been assigned to me and I was to see to her needs for the day and handle all new orders, etc. I was to take her to Dr. Patel's office, where she would be interviewed by him. I was not looking forward to this task as Dr. Patel was very quiet, or soft-spoken, and had a thick African accent, which I often found hard to understand. He was a nice fellow, just hard to understand. Anyway, I escorted Sarah to his office. We sat there in the hot, confined little office for what seemed like hours, but was actually about 30 minutes. The doctor reviewed many things about the patient's symptoms. "Are you hearing voices?" "Are you seeing things that aren't really there?" "Do you feel like harming yourself"? These are pretty standard questions to ask someone who suffers from schizophrenia.

The patient yelled at him, "I am pregnant and the baby is overdue. I need a C-section!" Dr Patel asked, "How long have you been pregnant?" to which Sarah replied, "Three and a half years." Dr. Patel shook his head and told the patient that she was not pregnant, and that she was just imagining it. He reminded her that her illness can cause a person to hallucinate or suffer delusions. Hallucinations occur when a person's brain chemistry becomes out of balance, and fools them, so to speak. It is when we see something that isn't really there—shadows or people, etc.—or we hear someone talking to us, but there isn't actually anyone else in the room. Basically, when any of our five senses are mixed up, a person can misinterpret something and believe it to be real when it is not. So, in a sense, our brain fools us. A delusion is when we believe something to be true, but only we believe it; the bulk of society would not. For example, a delusion would be if a person thinks they can cure cancer with positive thought—that is clearly a delusion. If a person believes they have to stay at least three feet away from everyone else's head or that person will steal their thoughts, that would also be an example of a delusion.

Sarah had, unfortunately, suffered from both hallucinations and delusions for many years, as a result of her schizophrenia. Dr. Patel knew this, and he also knew she could not be pregnant for three and a half years, and that she had terminated a pregnancy many years ago. She had been engulfed with guilt over that, and at one point attempted a failed suicide because of the guilt she carried for "killing her baby." Sometimes when a person has had a traumatic experience in real life, like having the abortion was for Sarah, they can incorporate it into their delusion. This was the angle that we had to work on with Sarah. We had to keep reassuring her that she was not really pregnant, remind her that a pregnancy test had been done and that it was negative. You can't just tell someone with schizophrenia the truth, or the reality of a situation, and expect them to readily understand that reality and accept it, as the delusions they have are extremely real to them. All you can do is keep presenting reality by way of different types of therapy, one of which is cognitive behavior therapy, or CBT, which had been done with Sarah in the past, but clearly it had not taken care of all of her delusions.

Dr. Patel explored with the patient her guilt at having had an abortion in the past, and asked her if she was feeling guilty about that, to open up a dialogue. She said, "Yes, but that's not what this is; I need an emergency C-section—I have been pregnant for over three years." Dr. Patel once again tried to introduce reality to the patient by explaining the normal gestation time for a human. At that point Sarah screamed, "I'm not fucking retarded, I know that; that's why I'm worried. I'm way overdue." Dr. Patel again tried to calm the patient and finished explaining the process, which Sarah listened to as she was biting her lip and rocking ever so slightly back and forth in the chair. When finished he said, "I want to schedule in some therapy sessions with you this week." Sarah said, "Fine," and Dr. Patel seemed relieved. He had calmed her down for now, and she had stopped insisting she was pregnant. He then went over her medications, and asked if she had been taking any additional drugs or alcohol, as this is a big no-no for anyone with a mental illness. It makes them way more ill, and very fast. As Dr. Patel was getting up out his chair, he said, "Well, if there isn't anything else . . . " Sarah interrupted him and said, "So when will I get my C-section?" Dr. Patel raised his gaze to the ceiling and said, "Sarah, you are not pregnant, there is no possible way you are pregnant. We have tested you—you're NOT PREGNANT." Sarah began to raise her voice, and said, "Yes I am. Why do I have breast milk then?" Dr. Patel again sat down, and started to explain to Sarah, "It is a delusion you are suffering from. You can't be pregnant for three and a half years, and if you're not pregnant or nursing a baby, you can't have breast milk, period."

Sarah glared at him for about five seconds and appeared very angry, then she stood up quickly, pulled her shirt up over her breasts, and squeezed out a perfect stream of breast milk across the table, hitting Dr. Patel in the face and chest with it. I was shocked to say the least, but not as much as Dr. Patel. For a second, I thought he was going to turn white with fear. He looked horrified, not surprised. He was always a bit of a wimp, and probably thought he had been assaulted.

I spoke up and said, "Well, Sarah, there is definitely something going on . . . I certainly believe that. The doctor and I will talk about it and try and come up with some answers for you. We can meet after lunch." Dr. Patel still looked like he'd had a bag of snakes dumped on his lap, but he nodded his head, and said, "Yes, let's do that."

This poor woman, who was clinically psychotic, I now realized had a very good reason that would make her feel as though she was pregnant. Remember, I said certain things that happen in real life can feed into one's delusions. How could this woman, who was rarely clear in her thinking, not think that she was pregnant? She clearly was producing breast milk and had a visible belly that had grown in the last couple of years. It was not hard to see why she would think she was overdue and so stressed out about the whole thing.

It was the talk of the nursing station, what had just happened, and now we wanted answers, too, as to how Sarah was producing milk. After a thorough investigation of all the patient medications, we discovered that her new antipsychotic that she had been placed on, called Resperidone, which was relatively new on the market, could cause people to lactate, and in males, even cause their breasts to enlarge. It also causes patients to become very hungry and most give in to the hunger and eat and eat and eat, and in some cases have been known to gain as much as 100 lbs. This could also explain Sarah's huge belly.

Sarah did much better in the weeks to come as we transitioned her to another antipsychotic. That was probably about 25 years ago, and I can still see the shocked look on Dr. Patel's face every time I pour a Resperidone table for a patient. I often laugh about it while dispensing medications. But I have never laughed about the horrible situation that Sarah was experiencing. For over three years she suffered needlessly because no one asked the right questions and assumed her complaints were just those of a psychotic, delusional patient.

We need to do better.

Work-Related Injuries

There are many jobs that aren't exactly safe, but people still have to do them every day. I believe, if most people were to guess which jobs are the most dangerous, they would say: construction worker, firefighter, police, military, etc. Well, I firmly believe that working as a nurse, especially a psychiatric nurse, is just as dangerous, if not more dangerous, than any other profession in North America. The OSHA, Occupational Safety and Health Administration, has a lot of data on this that supports what I am saying. They are constantly coming up with new and improved guidelines to help people in the workplace stay safe, but injuries will always be inevitable.

When a person is in training as a nurse, they are taught proper techniques to lift people, how to bend at the knees, get a second person to help them lift, use the various apparatuses that are available in some cases to aid in lifting, etc. Yet, all of that is just not enough, and nursing staff get injured all the time. Sometimes it can be avoided, but much of the time, it is just the nature of the job. If you're a nurse, you're most likely not going to be able to avoid a back injury, just as if you're a carpet layer, your knees will suffer badly. An electrician will get arthritis in his/her hands, a painter will have a bad neck from looking up at a ceiling all the time, and so on. Each job comes with its own common types of stressors or injuries. But nursing takes the cake; it is riddled with a plethora of permanent injuries that one can get.

I remember a co-worker who brandished a nice big scar in the palm of his hand where a knife was plunged straight through to the other side by an angry patient. The reason the knife went through his hand was because he raised his hand to cover his face as the patient attacked him, during supper, in the ward dining room.

That's not something you're taught to do in school: protect your face from a knife attack. To make matters worse, the staff member, after being stabbed and making a trip to the emergency room, had to work with the same patient the very next day. Management did not bother to intervene, nor did the doctor. My friend should not have had to work with that patient again. The patient could have easily been moved to another unit. The nurse's psychological well-being or personal safety was not taken into consideration—no surprise there.

Another night, a code was called and we all rushed to the psychiatric rehabilitation unit, where a combative patient had stabbed the nursing supervisor in the throat with a pencil. The patient only drew a bit of blood, and a couple of large Band-Aids were all that was needed to stop the bleeding. Maybe the fact that the nursing supervisor did not die is why the doctor would only lock the patient in the seclusion room for a few hours, and then let her out again to roam free about the ward at 8:00 the next morning, contrary to the nursing staff's objections.

The doctor wrote the order to release her after he was done on the unit and had time to leave. After all, she was dangerous and he knew it, but he wanted to test out the patient's anger on the nursing staff, to see if she would behave. He didn't want to put himself in harm's way. Nobody liked this doctor; he was always pulling this type of move. He was, for lack of a better word, an asshole.

One bright, sunny spring day, a co-worker was assigned to do a home visit with an individual who was now in the community after being on a psychiatric unit for many years. He was very ill and could not help the fact that he was born with a mental illness, but this did not mean he wasn't dangerous, and he had, in fact, injured many staff over the years. My co-worker went to his apartment and rang the bell. This very large man, about 6'4" and 260 lbs, opened the door and let her in. She was supposed to give him his antipsychotic medication by way of an intramuscular injection, which he had been receiving every three weeks for a number of years. Bruce, however, had other ideas. He said, "I want to have sex with you. Let's have sex now—that's why you're here, right?" Cindy was terrified, as the patient had just slammed the door and was standing between her and the only visible means of escape. As he moved closer, he asked her to take her clothes off and said again, "Let's have sex." Cindy managed to remain calm enough to say, "I should use the bathroom first." Bruce showed her where the bathroom was, she went inside and locked the door, and quickly opened the window and crawled out onto the roof, and jumped down to the ground.

She managed to get away with only a sprained ankle and was safe. Her ankle, over time, was fine, but can you imagine what this did to my co-worker's state of mind? How would this affect her, quite possibly for the rest of her life? We need a system that protects nursing staff better than this. The patient's doctor helped this situation by writing an order that, when staff went to visit this patient, they were not to visit him alone, but rather two staff were always to attend due to safety concerns. By the way, my saying that the "doctor helped" was sarcasm on my part, in case you missed it. How could he write such an order? If the patient was that dangerous with staff, then he was obviously dangerous to the general public, and the doctor should have written an order to bring him back to the hospital for a thorough evaluation. That shit goes on all the time. How safe would you feel with this man living beside you, or your daughter or sister? I would want to move my daughter to another state.

Another nurse that I worked with for many years was making the rounds one afternoon, when a disgruntled patient, who was also psychotic, decided that he would attack my friend. He, for no apparent reason, punched him several times in the head and chest, rendering him unconscious. Andy was one of the kindest nurses I've ever known. He was a hard worker and always did all that he could for his patients, but his jaw was busted, regardless of that.

Andy was off work for several months, recuperating, but when he got back to work, the patient was still on his unit. I can only imagine how I would feel coming back to work after such a severe beating and having to work with the same individual again. We did manage to transfer the patient later that day, and keep my friend out of danger. But, amazingly enough, they started bringing that very patient, who beat up my friend and co-worker, back to our unit for group therapy, later that same week. Andy's face turned as red as the hair on his head when he saw the patient walk onto the unit.

The harm to my friend was minimized by management again. What the hell is wrong with people? Should it not be basic common sense that if someone beats a person unconscious and breaks their jaw, that that person should never have to work with that patient again, as they very well might take another beating from them? Also, psychologically, should that nurse have to endure further unnecessary hardship? Fuck no, they shouldn't; it's pretty simple. Andy was never right after that. Years later he was still having headaches and sleep problems. Most people don't routinely get the shit beat out of them at work, nor are they prepared to deal with it when it does happen. They should be receiving support from their employer, even compensation. Instead, Andy had to wait a few months to get paid workers' compensation for the shifts he missed. It's a horrible system.

Another young friend of mine had his share of skirmishes at the local psychiatric unit. One day while rushing to a code, he entered a patient's room to find the patient kneeling on a young female nurse, choking her with one hand and trying to hit her with the other. Terry and two other staff intervened. As they were holding the patient on the ground, on his back, the patient began to spit at Terry and tried to bite him. Terry had ahold of him with both hands, trying to pin him to the ground, pushing down on each shoulder. The man kept lurching upward and trying to bite Terry. Terry held him down tight, for fear of being bitten, as he knew the patient who was intentionally trying to bite him had AIDS. He had been charged with attempting to infect another person on the street in a similar fashion. That day,

Terry ripped both shoulders, messed up both rotor cuffs. He hasn't been the same since. Long story short, 15 years later, his shoulders still cause him grief. He didn't receive any compensation from that incident, just ridicule from upper management, who told him he should get more help and protect himself in these situations. I bet he was close to smashing them in the mouth when they talked to him like that. If someone at your place of employment tried to bite you to give you AIDS, how would your manager react?

I could go on and on, talking about every fight I have been in, but you get the point. I myself have probably been in a hundred fights. That's not just a round figure I pulled out of the air. When I say fights, I mean times I had to subdue a patient, or pull them off another staff member before they killed them or beat them half to death. It happens! I would be in one of these fights or wrestling matches about every other week on average, sometimes two or three in one day—multiply that by 30 years. No wonder I look like I do. I have personally strained my shoulder, both knees, an ankle, received an abdominal tear that required surgery, fractured ribs, strained my back on too many occasions to count, had a concussion, a herniated disc . . . I've had most of my body bruised and wounded at one time or another. On one particular day, a young lad beat me pretty badly and I received about eight kicks and 13 punches. He was 6'10" tall to my 5'6". He was also a black belt in karate and as I, too, have been trained in martial arts, I recognized his abilities. My personal training came in handy. I'm sure I didn't look very graceful in the fight I put up defending myself when the patient attacked and tried to kill me, but I did enough to stay alive. I honestly don't think I would have made it, had I not trained in martial arts for so many years as a kid.

Now remember, I said I was a registered nurse. When a person is thinking about enrolling in school to be a nurse, would they be aware that all of the above is part of the job? Would it be in the brochure? I think not. I sure as hell wasn't.

The Reverend Without Compassion

From the time we are little, a great many of us are raised to believe that the local reverend, priest, rabbi, imam, or whatever you call your religious leader, is more morally grounded than the rest of us and has a deeper love of people, is more compassionate, etc. What happens when a religious leader does not live up to the high standards we expect, or when they fall short of those standards miserably?

When I was still a fairly green nurse, I was beginning another busy afternoon shift on a medical-surgical unit in Texas. While I was making my preliminary rounds and checking in with my floor nurses, I heard a commotion coming from a room a couple doors down the hall. I heard a man yelling, "Get out of here, you filthy little [N-word] bitch," and then I saw a young nursing aide who was Black, quickly leaving the room as a box of Kleenex hit her on the back.

I immediately asked her what had just happened. I could see she was visibly upset. She proceeded to tell me, "It's okay, he just doesn't want me in his room on account of I'm colored, it's okay," to which I said, "No, it's not okay."

I entered the room and the patient was scowling. He said, "Thank the Lord that you are here, I just need to potty. Can you help me to get to the commode?"

As I bit my lip, he said, "Keep that little [N-word] girl out of my room. I don't want one of those filthy things near me. You can look after me okay, Jack?"

Now, I knew all about racism and all the horrible things that went along with it, but I had never been witness to this kind of abuse up close, and been in a position that I was both duty-bound and morally bound to intervene. Wow, what a dilemma. I was a new employee, in a state where racism was pervasive, and the patient—a reverend, no less—was a good paying client of the hospital's. No matter what

I did next, I did not see things going well for me. So, I had a frank discussion with the good reverend.

I informed my racist patient that I was the charge nurse on the unit, and that meant I had a lot of other duties to perform, and taking people to the bathroom was not one of them, and that it was the nurse tech's job. I said, "When you ring your bell, if I am not busy doing the things I am responsible for, I will gladly help you, but chances are you will have to wait a long time, as my job is very demanding and there are a lot of things, emergency-type things, that happen on a medical-surgical unit such as this one." The reverend said, "That's okay, Jack, I understand, but I would rather wait a little longer for you, than have one of them tend to me." I said "Okay, Reverend," and left the room just at the time his nurse was bringing in his dose of magnesium citrate drink. For those of you who don't know what this is, it's a tasty drink that makes one have to evacuate their bowels very quickly. It is often given as a last resort, when someone can't have a bowel movement, or when the alternative is to have an obstruction so bad that they will either have a ruptured bowel or require surgery. In some cases it's used to clean out the bowel before surgery. So, in layperson's terms, it's going to make you run to the toilet, and fast.

So about 45 minutes later, our good reverend was ringing his bell, which I ignored as I was genuinely very busy. The bell continued to ring, and ring, and ring, for about an hour. Not once, twice, but three times our lovely nurse tech started to approach the patient's room, and I stopped her each time. She looked terribly worried and said, "It's okay, I don't mind, I'm used to it. Why don't you want me to go in?" I said, "He doesn't want you in his room because he is a racist asshole." She looked surprised for a few seconds. Then I saw her break into a smile, as she turned and went to another room to help someone who was not abusive toward her.

By that time, I had actually gotten caught up with my other work, so I proceeded to go and help the reverend, who at this point was sobbing. He was lying in his bed with shit running between his legs, down to the bottom of the mattress and onto the floor. He screamed at me, "Where were you? Where was everybody? I've been calling for almost two hours! I shit the bed." I said with a straight look on my face, "I'm sorry, Reverend, but I came like I said I would, as soon as I finished my work." He then said, "Well, couldn't anyone else come"? And I said "No, unfortunately there were just a couple of Black nurses, and I told them you had requested they never enter your room." He was very quiet the whole time that I took to clean him up, but at the end he said, "Please, just tell them to come in the next time." So, I did.

To my surprise, about an hour later as I passed by his room, I heard him say to the nurse tech, "I'm sorry, and I'm ashamed of the way I treated you. I don't expect you to ever forgive me." I just kept walking as I thought, "Oh shit, did I just do that? I could get fired for what I did," but he was a real asshole, so whatever. About a week later in report, one of the nurses informed me that the reverend had apologized to the rest of the Black staff to whom he had been abusive. She then handed me a note that the reverend had left for me. It read, "Dear Jack, thanks for the lesson in humanity. I will pray for you."

The next time you go to the hospital and others are in charge of your bowels, be nice.

Don't Eat That

Most of us have witnessed a dog eat vomit or feces, and it usually sickens us. We turn away in disgust, or if it is our pet, we scold it and are reluctant to let it near us for a while—and we certainly don't let it lick us. Dogs are animals; it's normal for such things to happen in the animal kingdom. We are also animals, but much higher functioning and aware of the dangers in ingesting this type of thing. Plus, it's just a horrible, disgusting thought. But what if a person has diminished cognitive ability? What then?

We have all seen many examples of babies or toddlers, who are just learning about the world around them and don't know what is appropriate and what is not to put in their mouths, do something gross. I remember my son at about 14 months of age. I was holding him on the picnic table on our back porch. He reached down and pulled a marble-sized piece of mud out of his shoe and popped it into his mouth before I could stop him. What happened next was hilarious. He took about two seconds to spit it out, and an awful look came over his face; he clearly did not enjoy the taste of the dirt. He was tearing up, and beginning to cry before the last of it had rolled off of his tongue. It was one of those memorable moments that you wish you could have captured on film. Unfortunately, not all moments are something we want to catch on film, yet they are very memorable—even if we would rather forget they ever happened.

One time I was working the day shift on a medium-secure psychiatric facility. On this particular unit, patients had privileges to use the grounds for recreation, unescorted by staff. Upon return to the unit, we nursing staff had to check each patient thoroughly for both contraband and weapons. As I was using a metal detector, held by hand, to check one patient before allowing him back onto the unit, I noticed he smelled badly. This was common on a schizophrenia unit, as a lot of patients refuse to bathe. The metal detector is used like a wand, and it has to be passed over the body about an inch from the patient, and we have to bend down to check their lower legs. While I was bending forward, I noticed the unmistakable smell of shit. I figured he either dirtied his pants or had not wiped properly. As I was passing the wand over his arms, the patient took a quick bite out of the chocolate bar he was holding in his right hand. As he straightened out his arm again, he nearly hit me with the chocolate bar.

"Holy fuck!" I said aloud, as I realized he was eating a piece of shit. He was holding it like a chocolate bar, and literally had a shit-eating grin. He was smiling and I could see all the feces in his teeth, as he then held the turd up to my face and said, "You want a bite, Jack"? I nearly puked right on the spot. I then thought to myself, *Is that his, or does it belong to someone else?* Somehow, it would be worse if it wasn't his. Clearly, I had worked there too long.

I knew this patient well. He was not doing this for attention; it was more that he could not fully appreciate what he was doing. He was actually at about the same cognitive level as a toddler, or a dog. His cognitive level was so reduced by his illness that he just did not understand the gravity of what he was actually doing. When well, he was a very nice, polite person, who would never act this way and would be embarrassed to see himself in his current condition.

Another day, while administering the noon medications, Ralph, another long-time resident who suffered from schizophrenia, approached the medication cart. As I handed him a Dixie cup full of water to swallow the medication I had given him, he declined and said, "I'm good," and showed me his plastic drink bottle of ginger ale. He then said, "This is better for me, it makes me strong. It's going to cure me and make me live forever." He swallowed his medication with a gulp of ginger ale, and only then did I notice it was in a Coke bottle.

I realized then, as I detected the stench of old urine—he was drinking piss. This was not the first patient we'd had do this. I don't know what it is, but plenty of delusional patients have been known to drink their own urine. Most believe it is good for them. If it wasn't so pathetic and sad, it would be laughable, to an extent.

I later went into Ralph's dorm and found one of those old red-and-blue Adidas gym bags, full of about 25 bottles of his urine. When I had just about finished getting rid of them, Ralph entered the bathroom and caught me pouring the last bottle of urine down the toilet. He was very angry and threatened to kill me for taking his life-saving elixir. He had to be placed in locked seclusion for three days until he calmed down enough so that we could safely let him out.

Ralph was one of many patients who was steered by his delusions. Others who partake in this type of behavior have a decreased cognitive ability, and sometimes both issues come into play. I have seen many patients regress like this, or fall to this level of thinking. Over the years, there have been too many to count.

I have seen patients nonchalantly reach down and pick up a piece of dog shit and eat it. Another time, a patient jumped headfirst into a 40-gallon drum of garbage, and ended up rolling down a 30-foot hill, while still inside the drum, and came out holding a handful of mostly eaten fried chicken, with a wing between his teeth. He then offered to share his find with myself and two other patients.

Witnessing these types of behaviors always makes me feel sad for the individual, and reminds me how unfair life can be for some of us.

Child Molesters and Rapists Aplenty

On one of the units on which I worked, we had a patient who had been deemed NCR, which means "not criminally responsible." In other words, he did not know that raping dozens and dozens of little boys was wrong. So, he did not have to go to a regular jail, but rather, was sent to a psychiatric hospital. Horseshit! On this particular unit, patients were being gradually reintegrated into the community. If they were good, they could receive privileges to walk on the hospital grounds, by themselves, gradually earning more and more time off the unit, unsupervised. Eventually they could go downtown, get a job, and finally get their own apartment.

This particular individual, who had a long list of children that he had molested, was now working in the community, going door-to-door delivering items, all day long. He did have to report back to the unit at night. Now, while these patients are earning their way up to this point, and for a long time after, we don't just take their word for it that they are where they say they are going to be. They have to fill out an itinerary, and we nursing staff have to go out, in an unmarked car, and do spot checks on them. If they are not where they are supposed to be, they usually have their privileges revoked and have to start over, depending on their doctor and what their warrant states about the parameters of their reintegrating into society.

One day, a staff member who was driving by a park saw this individual playing with some minors. This was not allowed, as stated by his warrant, as these were the very people he tended to molest. The staff member reported it to the unit and to the doctor. He was informed by the patient's doctor, "Don't lie about our patients." You read it right. Stop and think about that: A child molester who had molested dozens of kids was seen playing with kids, unaccompanied by an adult, at a park, and the staff member was accused of lying. You better hope your kids don't play in that park. Another pathetic flaw in the system.

The patient, after this event, graduated to being able to have his own apartment. He was also allowed to buy another van with curtains on it, and a brand-new puppy, to basically set up exactly the way he was when he molested his first dozen victims after luring them into the van to pet the puppy. All of this, the entire treatment team was aware of, including the doctor.

I never could figure out why that particular doctor was that reckless, and so easily prone to believing the patient over staff members. I don't have a beef with all doctors, in case you're wondering. Some are fantastic, but not this particular doctor. He was always an asshole, right to the end when he finally retired. They could have had his going-away cake and tea in the patients' phone booth.

Who wants pizza? Well, most everybody enjoys a pizza on a Saturday night after a long week at either work or school. One of my co-workers ordered a pizza one Saturday night for her family, in which there were two young children. When the doorbell rang about 30 minutes later, she and the children, who were very excited, went to the door. Her smile quickly turned to shock as she opened the door and saw Jamie, our long-time pedophile, who had just recently started a new job in the community, unbeknownst to her. She was in shock. She paid for the pizza, trying to be pleasant, while shielding her two young children from the leering pedophile. She told us, "After I closed the door, I almost puked right there. Instead, I went into the bathroom and cried." The problem now was he knew where she lived, knew she had young children, and was out on the street and could ostensibly show up there at any time and take her kids. It was a predicament we saw far too often, working with these types of criminals who are supposedly too ill to realize it's wrong to molest children. There was nothing she could do; he had not done anything wrong. He was allowed by law to go out and get a job, and until he did molest her children, or attempt to, there was simply nothing she could do.

One of the things you have to realize is that we piss off a lot of these guys while they are in the hospital. For example, if they fail a drug test that we administer, they lose their privileges and blame us. If they deviate from their itinerary that they are supposed to follow when first being allowed to go into the community, and we, one of the nurses, catch them and report it, they become very angry with us. So, you see, we make a lot of enemies doing the job we do. We definitely don't want a child molester targeting our kids in any type of revenge scenario, which has happened.

Think twice before you order take-out, and never allow your children to go to the door—make them set the table or something, instead.

Occupational therapy refers to when a person who has experienced a major health problem takes on some type of work. The goal in having patients do these jobs is not so much about making money, as it is about helping the patient reintegrate into society, develop new skills, and increase their self-esteem and self-worth. This is a great idea in most cases, but can be disastrous in others.

We had a 43-year-old patient, a white male, about 5'6" tall, who had a very low IQ and was also deemed mentally ill and had an impulse control disorder. This meant that he easily became angered and would lash out, hurting or destroying anyone in his path with very little warning, if any at all. Any one of these issues is deeply debilitating, let alone all of the issues combined.

There were a lot of jobs around the hospital that this individual could do, and he did benefit from doing them. What I, and the majority of staff, disagreed with were the doctor's orders, and the law, which advocated placing this individual in the community—due to the fact that this person had been previously convicted of molesting two little boys and then murdering them. This is what his offence was, one he'd committed just a few years prior to being placed in the community on a work program. Nursing staff for the most part don't like allowing this type of individual off the property at all. But, the powers that be had decided it was a good idea for him to attend the local college and take a food prep course, and then get a job in a restaurant. This meant that he would have all kinds of access to young children, and staff would not be there nearly often enough to monitor him and make sure he did not take a notion to murder or molest another child. Doesn't that whole sentence just sound pathetic? It almost seems like something made up. Sadly, this happens all the time: guys like this are allowed to re-integrate into the community to both work and prey on the weak and vulnerable, sexually assaulting people again. There is very little we can do about it.

This individual did eventually get a job at a restaurant, at which all staff immediately stopped eating. He did fairly well, and even made friends with some of the patrons. How do I know this? Well, we received a call from a concerned citizen who let us know, "One of your guys is down here and I don't think he should be near little kids but he's babysitting them." It turned out that Mikey had made friends with a young single mother with two small boys who frequented the restaurant, and she required a babysitter from time to time. Mikey to the rescue! He volunteered to watch the children in the daytime, as he had to report back to the psychiatric hospital every evening after work.

What do you suppose happened to this individual, when both staff and his doctor found out about his babysitting gig? Even though he clearly had it written on his warrant that he must never be alone and unaccompanied around children? Well, he was given a stern warning from his doctor, and then he went to work the next day. There should have been a thorough investigation to learn what had actually taken place with those children, if they were abused, hurt, or threatened in any way. We will never know. This kind of thing goes on all the time. It's pathetic, and criminal.

I am not against patients reintegrating into the community and taking jobs; it's actually a good idea for some. But if you own a restaurant, and you take a chance on a psychiatric patient or former inmate working at your establishment, it might just be a good idea to ask what exactly they were charged with, and if they are reluctant to tell you . . . need I say more? Don't get me wrong; some of these former patients and inmates are awesome. I know one prison that puts out better chefs than most of the cooking schools; they are fully trained and I have no problem eating at the restaurants that hire them. Once again, it all comes down to common sense, who should be allowed to work in the community. This patient I was speaking of raped and killed little boys, and his cognitive ability had not increased with his time in the hospital, and I don't believe his attraction to murdering and molesting kids had changed either. Think about it.

I saw many other psychiatric patients over the years who had committed rape, more than once, and not while under the influence of drugs or alcohol, either. They all eventually got out and would eventually get their own apartment, and many ended up committing rape again.

Most people reading this will be deeply disturbed. I agree; it's repulsive. But in each and every case I am aware of, had the nursing staff had their way, these individuals never would have been allowed off the hospital grounds without staff supervision. Our system is severely flawed and does not serve to protect society as much as a psychiatric patient's rights. Which, I believe, is nothing short of criminal.

Parents, protect your children; it's more dangerous out there than most people realize.

Christmas Cheer

Christmas is a great time of year, along with New Year's Eve. It's a social time that makes a lot of people happy and giddy, but not everyone. I used to notice that some of the bitchy nurses were easier to get along with around the holidays, but others were just miserable. Sometimes a little Christmas cheer helps us be more friendly—or at least, put up with those who refuse to be.

I knew one colleague who was always quiet during the first part of the day and perked up later in the afternoon. I made mention of this one day to another staff member. She said, "No shit, why do you think that is?" Apparently, he was going to lunch every day and hitting "Rusti's Roadhouse" for two or three beers, or sometimes would just sit in his car and have a couple of pints. She went on to tell me, "He's drunk here every day, and has three or four on the way home." As time went on, I started to notice that he was drunk by the end of shift. I felt a little foolish that I had not picked up on this earlier on my own. Then one day, out of the blue, in the nursing station, he was complaining about the police doing random checks for impaired drivers. He mentioned that he had been lucky to not have gotten a DWI on the way to work that night, as the police were apparently just ending the spot checks as he was pulling up to the cruiser. He said, "They waved me through and then peeled out of there themselves—must have had an emergency." Keep in mind he was driving to work and was already impaired. He would give you substandard care for sure, working as a registered nurse. He eventually ended up getting fired, but that was because the police came to the unit and arrested him in front of all his peers and patients. They then walked him out in handcuffs. I believe he was stalking his ex-wife, and she was dating a state trooper so that took care of him. I had always wondered why he was such a useless nurse. I guess it was the drinking, for the most part.

Another fellow I worked with would go to the patients' TV room every night after report and sit with the psychiatric patients to monitor them. Someone had to be on the unit, and it might as well be Chuck. Chuck was a 47-year-old male nurse, overweight and overbearing, and an asshole most of the time. He elected to take that post as he had a bottle of whiskey behind the fire extinguisher casing that he always left there. He would remove the two screws on the panel every night, right in front of the patients. The patients would often go to the canteen on a run for him to buy Coke for him to use as mix. He would give them a little taste for their troubles. A lot of the older men who worked at this hospital were only hired to break up fights and lock up patients when they needed to be placed in seclusion, so they got away with this type of behavior: drinking on the job, etc. How they ever got through nursing school, I'll never know.

We had a manager one time who was pleasant one day and a bitch the other; we could never figure out what her mood was going to be like. She was hard to get to know and even harder to like. Management does bring with it a lot of stress, but she brought it on herself.

She finally got fired, like most managers did at that facility, and we all celebrated. I almost did a cartwheel down the hall, but didn't want to be to unprofessional, and I never learned how to do one, anyway. When they cleaned out her office, after she had been walked out of the building, they found about a half-dozen liquor bottles. Then we knew why she was so hit and miss, as far as her moods went.

Another time on a maximum-secure psychiatric unit, I was working the night shift on New Year's Eve with a group of co-workers who didn't let the fact that they were working stop them from having a good time. After the patients were in bed, the party favors came out and so did the alcohol. There was hard liquor, whiskey, rum and two kinds of gin. A makeshift bar was set up on the medication cart. It was hard to believe what I was seeing. When the nursing supervisor showed up, he knew exactly what was going on, and he just said, "Be careful, don't drink too much of that Coke," and then left. Looking back, I think he was probably part of the original party crew himself, having worked on the unit with most of the staff for many years before moving over to management.

Before the night was over, Brenda, one of the senior nurses, was starting to feel sick. I walked into the medication room to find her bent over the med cart, with her jeans and panties at her ankles, as our colleague Fred administered a shot of intramuscular Gravol into her butt. Gravol is an anti-emetic, after all, and great at controlling nausea. I immediately left the medication room, and stayed as far away from that scene as I could.

The next day, the day staff could smell the booze in the nursing station, as it was on the night staff's breath. The empty cups that had contained the mixed drinks had been thrown into the trash in the same small office. One of the day nurses pulled out a bra from behind the cushion of the sofa chair. She said, "Well, it looks like someone had a good night." I responded with, "It sure wasn't me." Just then another nurse pulled out one of the rolling chairs to take a seat and get ready for report, but something was dragging on the wheel of the chair and streaking a mess across the floor. As she reached down to pick it up, she squealed, "Oh, fuck me," as she flicked away what was a spent condom, and she had just had it in her hand. It landed on the report table. She stood up then and said, "You fucking dirty pigs, it's like a whorehouse in here," and she stomped off to the other room.

It was pretty bad and made for a tense couple of weeks, until another employee got caught accidentally kissing a patient. There was a big inquiry, and that took people's minds off the New Year's Eve party that had gone amok.

You Must Not Have Sex with the Patients

Most people know that it is not appropriate for health care workers to have sex with patients who are under their care. Health care workers certainly know this. So, to hear a nurse on a psychiatric unit lecture a couple of student nurses on this topic seemed a little overboard to the rest of us. Kenny was always thorough and thought of himself as a bit of an expert on everything; he would often be heard giving unsolicited advice to the new students. Apparently, they should have had Kenny go around to the other units, too, when the new students arrived from the local university to start their placement with us. On the floor above us, one of the students had become romantically involved with a patient. All hell broke loose—there was an investigation and the kid was dismissed from her placement. The school's intern program at our facility was now in jeopardy. It was a big mess, to say the least.

I witnessed many examples of this over my lifetime.

I once worked in a prison and one of the part-time nursing staff on our unit was obviously spending too much time with a certain inmate. Other staff had noticed this and warned her that it looked bad, took her aside and spoke to her, etc. Yet the problem persisted. She would let him break the rules of conduct that he was to abide by and turn a blind eye. She started bringing him contraband from the street, like magazines, newspapers, candy, and who knew what else. Luckily, the inmate was discharged, and that was one less problem to worry about.

Once the inmate was out in the community, more than one staff member saw the two of them together. They were seen holding hands at a dog track, a favorite meeting place for criminals. Staff reported this to management, but it was ignored like so many other things that should have been addressed over the years. A couple of months later, that same inmate was arrested and incarcerated yet again.

This was bad for us staff, as he was back on the same unit with the nurse that he was suspected of having relations with. This made things very uncomfortable for us, as we knew management was refusing to do anything about it. Staff were even reluctant to give a proper report about what had transpired the previous shift, for fear that this nurse would go right down the hall and inform him what the other nurses were saying about him. This was something that was very disturbing to the remainder of the staff. It was a big safety issue. We would give a guarded or abbreviated report to the rest of the staff, holding back any really dangerous information, and quietly whisper it to the oncoming team leader after the main report was given and the nurse was down the hall visiting the inmate she was having relations with.

Eventually, the inmate got out again, and the nurse moved right into his house with him. This pretty little brunette could have had anyone she wanted, but picked this scumbag who had a history of beating women. Sadly, she too, became a victim. She finally decided to move on.

To illustrate how common this type of thing is, I was working on another unit where some of the older nurses were compiling a list of all the staff they could think of who had been known to be having sex with inmates and psychiatric patients, or caught in compromising situations: in a closet, the back seat of a car in the employee parking lot, the inmate's bed, kneeling in front of them behind the dresser, etc. They were undecided whether it was 17 or 18. A pretty high number to say the least.

One of the most notorious instances involved a female psychologist who worked on a psychiatric unit with the patient she would become involved with and was acutely familiar with the heinous crimes that he had been charged with, and therefore incarcerated for. The psychologist had apparently fallen in love with this patient whom she had been treating for many years. She loved him so much that she left her husband, who also worked on the same unit as a nurse. She took their three little children with her and moved in with the patient upon his discharge. The husband was beside himself, terribly upset—who wouldn't be? He was not only suffering the loss of his family, but his wife had taken their kids to live with this very dangerous psychopath, who had already killed his previous wife. He was genuinely afraid for his kids, but if he went to the police and divulged that his kids were in danger and why, he could have been arrested for breach of confidentiality and defamation of character. Staff thought for sure he would kill this man if he saw him on the street, but if he did, he would go to prison for the rest of his life. He didn't need a gun—he was as big as a tree, looked a bit like Mike Tyson, too. I figured he would lose it and kill the guy with his bare hands if he ever got the chance. I would often look down the street that our misguided psychologist and her new flame lived on to see if the police were parked in front of their house, but they never were. This man's kids would call him from their new house to talk to him and this psychopath could be heard screaming obscenities at his ex-wife. This woman who left her husband and took their kids managed to keep her job doing therapy. In fact, her job was never even in jeopardy. You're probably asking yourself, how can this happen? Well, it happens all the time, and it's not like nursing staff don't complain and report these things. But management has a way of ignoring things, putting them off, or dealing with them in a half-assed manner.

There was another patient on the psychiatric rehab unit, Phillis, who was a very promiscuous woman and also suffered from schizophrenia, a very serious illness that caused her to have delusions and talk to people who weren't really there. On top of all this she had been severely sexually abused by a family member for years as a child. She would often get visits from a nurse who worked several buildings over, across the street at another location. He had keys to all the buildings in the complex, just like we all did, to enable us to be pulled to other units when they were short-handed, or respond to a Code 99 to help with a combatant patient. But this particular nurse began showing up a little too often on the unit. He would be seen talking to this patient at the patient canteen, or sometimes in her room sitting on her bed. She would be seen bringing big bags of candy back to the unit and would say, "My friend Tim gave it to me; he likes me and I'm nice to him, so he buys me things." Nobody ever caught them in the act, but there was no reason under the sun for him to be there so often, and it was a definite no-no to be giving gifts such as candy to patients, and especially to one patient in particular. Even if he had not been having sex with her, no man who has been a nurse would set himself up in such an awkward situation, to be scrutinized by all the other staff. The other patients even referred to Tim as Phillis's boyfriend.

Another time, a nurse who was thought to be having an affair or some type of inappropriate relations with a patient had been off work indefinitely, due to a recent work-related back injury. This must have been too much for her to handle, and she felt the need to seek some comfort from her clandestine lover.

One night the patient came up to the nursing station and said, "Sally hurt herself. She's in the stairwell." The nursing staff were initially puzzled as Sally was off on sick leave. But, sure enough, it was Sally lying at the bottom of the stairwell; she had slipped on something and fell the better part of a flight of stairs, breaking her leg. She had missed her inappropriately chosen lover, waited until 2:00 a.m. when she thought most of the staff would be sleeping in front of the television, and came up the back stairs to have a rendezvous with her man, our long-term resident pyromaniac. She was genuinely hurt now; I've often wondered if she claimed workers' compensation for that fall . . . it did happen at work, after all!

Constipation

It's not a glamourous topic, but it is a very real medical problem. Many people suffer from this issue. Lots of things can contribute to it, like pain meds, surgery, immobility, etc. It's not just an inconvenience; if left untreated, it can cause a lot of pain and misery—even a ruptured bowel requiring surgery. In hospitals many people are not able to keep track of their bowel movements due to sickness or decreased cognitive ability. It's no laughing matter.

I started a new job one time on a psychiatric unit. It was a specialty unit, catering to dual diagnosis patients. This meant that the patients were both mentally handicapped and also suffering from some form of mental illness; for example, schizophrenia, bipolar disorder, and so on.

After report one day, the head nurse informed me, "We have a young man here who has been constipated in the past and we don't believe he has had a bowel movement for a few days. The doctor has ordered a digital exam. The patient probably won't be happy; sometimes he resists us and it takes several men to safely do a digital on him. Just try your best with him and let us know if you need some help. He does require a firm approach. We can't take no for an answer, or he will end up in an awful mess."

Many of you would be appalled to know that sometimes we have to be somewhat forceful with these types of patients. You have to remember that they sometimes have not developed mentally beyond the level of a three-year-old. So, a quick finger in the bum is more humane than surgery for a ruptured bowel. But, understandably, no one likes a finger in the bum, regardless of your cognitive ability.

Elaine, the head nurse, pointed to the patient who was standing at the half-door, which was closed to the office. The patient was standing there with some other patients looking over the half-door into the office, eagerly waiting for report to finish, so they could get the cookie promised to them. When Elaine pointed toward the door and the patient, he waved at me with a big grin on his face. He would not be grinning for long. He was about 5'3", weighed about 260 lbs and was wearing a blue-and-yellow horizontal-striped shirt with chocolate ice-cream and mustard stains on it. This was not an uncommon look for this type of psychiatric patient, as they had to wear whatever clothes they could find from the hand-me-down bin most of the time.

After report was over, I approached the patient and said, "Hey buddy, we have to do a little procedure. Can you come with me?" He said, "Sure, need my help? I'm a good helper." He then donned that big grin again. He was probably feeling great, thinking he was helping the staff. It would often make a patient's day when they felt useful. I led him into the bathroom stall as I had been instructed. He said, "What'ya doing?" and I said, "You haven't had a poop in a long time, have you?" He said, "What do you mean?" And I responded, "You haven't pooped in a long time; we need to help you. Dr. Gonzales wants me to check your bum." My new chubby friend looked a little nervous, as he stammered, "What—what do you mean? I'm okay." And I had to tell him, "No, let me check your bum—off with the pants." I started to reach for his belt and then Elaine came running into the bathroom, yelling, "Jack, Jack, no, stop! Come here—stop." I left the patient and went out of the bathroom with her and she looked both horrified, and as though she was constipated herself, her face was so red. She then told me, "That's the wrong guy—he's the student social worker."

"Holy fuck," I said aloud. I do that a lot. *I almost stuck my finger up a student's ass.* Elaine was, by that time, bent over, attempting to stifle a laugh with tears running down her face. Even she, who was always so professional, could not stop laughing. But it wasn't really a laughing matter. If I had forced my finger into that student's rectum, I would have been in a lot of shit—literally and figuratively.

I remember another time we had a post-operative patient who had not had a bowel movement in a few days. He was in a lot of pain. Oral laxatives, and even a fleet enema, had not helped this process along. Now orders were received to give the patient a soap suds enema. This is when we hang a large bag of water filled with soap in it and run it into a person's bowels through a tube. It's no fun for the nurses or the patient, but it often works. I met up with his nurse in the patient's room to assist with the procedure, as the man was already sitting on the bedside commode. Ideally, this soap suds enema should be given while lying on your left side, but the patient was in extreme pain and his nurse had told him that we could try it while he sat on the commode chair. Which is basically a toilet seat with a bucket under it.

Todd said, "You lift him up a bit and I will remove the bucket and put the tube in, and once the enema is in, I will slide the bucket back." Easy for him to say; the man weighed about 250 lbs. Anyway, I hoisted him up with the patient's help. I could see Todd down through the toilet seat. At one point he was actually lying on his back looking up at the man's rear end, like a mechanic.

I released the clamps and allowed the soap suds enema to run into the man's rectum when given the nod from Nurse Todd. Naturally, we instructed the patient to hold it in. I told Todd, "You better get out from under there." He said, "Almost done." Just then, I could see his eyeballs widen as he attempted to scramble out from under the commode.

Needless to say, the man exploded and evacuated his bowels all over Todd. Todd was frantically hunting for a towel to wipe his face off as he yelled, "Fuck! Fuck, that was stupid! I'm covered in shit! Fuck me!" He then turned to the man and attempted to apologize for the outburst of profanity, but as he did, both the patient and I broke into laughter. I think we woke up half of the patients on the unit, as it was only 5:30 in the morning.

At the beginning of this story I said that constipation is no laughing matter, but maybe sometimes it is— unless you happen to be Todd.

Dextrocardia

Most of us joke a bit with our co-workers from time to time. Sometimes we even play pranks on them, especially those who deserve it because they've pulled one over on us.

I was the head nurse for a while on a medical-surgical unit. I had worked with most of my staff for long enough to know who I could tease and who I couldn't.

An apical heart rate is calculated when we use our stethoscope to listen directly to your heart. In this situation, we place the stethoscope over the apex of your heart. Doctors will order a heart rate to be obtained this way for various reasons, but mainly because it's more accurate.

As a head nurse, I never yelled at my staff or was hard to get along with. I was very understanding and soft-spoken most of the time. So, if I raised my voice and projected it down the hallway, staff knew it was important and, if possible, they would drop what they were doing and lend a hand. I might have abused my authority on this day a little bit, but I needed to pull one over on Debbie. She had been winning at that game lately.

As Debbie came out of a patient's room, I was holding the telephone receiver in one hand as I covered the mouthpiece with the other. I yelled, "Debbie, Dr. Hernandez needs an apical on 54 right away!" I was referring to the apical heart rate. Debbie, who was a great nurse, bolted to Room 54, where Mrs. Barber was sitting in a recliner chair beside her bed, reading a book. She was post-left-knee replacement. Debbie, who had entered the room about two minutes ago, was now standing beside Mrs. Barber with her stethoscope in her ears and she tapped so hard on the tympanum, the big round part, that she almost jumped out of her shoes. She was obviously having trouble hearing the heart rate.

By this time, I was standing at the door to Mrs. Barber's room. Debbie looked up and said, "I'm sorry, I don't know what's wrong. I'm having trouble hearing." I said, "Hurry, the doctor is waiting. You know what he gets like." She again placed the stethoscope over Mrs. Barber's left side of her chest, and measured again by counting ribs. She appeared uncertain as to where to place the stethoscope, a task that should be very easy. Debbie finally gave up and said, "I'm sorry. Can you do it? I'm embarrassed, but I'm having problems."

At this time Mrs. Barber said, "I guess she's not one of your brightest ones." Debbie looked like she had been slapped in the face. I said, "Sure, I'll do it," so I took her stethoscope from her and placed it on the right side of Mrs. Barber's chest, or sternum, and listened for a minute to her heart. I could see a bewildered look come over

Debbie's face and she then looked down at her own chest, touched her heart, looked at me, turned to face the same direction that Mrs. Barber was, and then slid her hand over to her right side and looked ever more confused.

I finished and informed Mrs. Barber, "No problems. Your heart rate is 76, same as your age. Your doctor just wanted to have us check. If you need anything, just ring the bell," to which Mrs. Barber replied, "Well, I won't be asking her for anything," as she directed a cold stare at Debbie for about five seconds. Then Mrs. Barber and I both broke out laughing.

Debbie looked that much more confused, in shock even, as she threw her hands slightly out to her sides with her palms facing up, as though she was surrendering, and said, "What the fuck is going on? I mean, what—sorry, I didn't mean to swear." Mrs. Barber piped up and said, "That's okay, dear. It's only fair—we were teasing you pretty bad. I have dextrocardia." After a few seconds, Debbie broke into laughter herself and actually had to bend over to get her breath. She than stood up and punched me in the chest—hard—and said, "You bastard!"

In case you haven't figured it out, dextrocardia is when a person's heart is on the wrong side; it's congenital, or you're born with it. Often, it can come with a bunch of other problems, but not always. In Mrs. Barber's case, it was just switched and had never caused her any major issues—and maybe even helped her develop a great sense of humor, or become a master prankster.

I then told Debbie how I had set this up with our patient the shift before. I quickly recognized what a hoot Mrs. Barber was and formulated a plan. Even I was surprised at how well she acted out the part—and the language she was capable of. Mrs. Barber and I played that trick on four different nurses and she had a ball every time. Not everything at the hospital has to be serious. When you get a chance to have some fun, go for it. It's healthy!

Hard to Witness

When people hear about a person who witnessed a horrific accident—a bloody scene where somebody died—they can understand how it would leave that person traumatized. We are more easily able to display empathy when dealing with people who may very well have been scarred for life. But not everything that wounds us emotionally is bloody and messy. Some things happen quietly without sirens and flashing lights and the presence of first responders.

When I was still very young myself, I had a patient only a few years older than I was. He was 32 and dying. I was a chemotherapy technician and had been seeing him for a couple of weeks. At first, he thought treatment would help him, or at least prolong his life—and when you're 32 years old and have a family, you want to take every day you can get.

I had gotten to know Jim over the few weeks that I had been caring for him. We had lots of frank talks about death and dying. He knew the score, so when he talked to me about his imminent demise, I didn't shower him with false hope and bullshit. That would be disrespectful and obvious. He talked a lot about his five-year-old son and what would become of him. Naturally, he was terribly upset that he would not see him grow up and play Little League, all that type of stuff. He also expressed how he felt guilty that he would not be around to provide for his son and wife financially, or to protect his son from the many things a father protects his kids. He even worried his wife would meet someone who would not treat her and his son well. That's a lot of shit for a dying man to worry about.

Jim's walls in his hospital room were plastered with crayon drawings his son would bring him each and every day. One day when I was finishing up a treatment, his son Jimmy Jr. came running in the room and dove onto his father's bed. I could tell the impact of his son landing on him hurt, as he was so weak and fragile by that time. He hugged little Jimmy anyway without complaint. My patient then sat on the edge of the bed and held his son in his lap. Little Jimmy was proudly showing his dad his latest masterpiece. I heard him say, "This is you and me fishing—you're helping me catch a big bass." Little Jimmy then turned to me and showed me the picture, no doubt to elicit more praise, which I gave him. He said, "My dad and I go to the river a lot to fish and we are going to go again in a couple days when Dad comes home. Are you going to be home this weekend, Dad? Can we go then? Mama can pack us a nice lunch, and we can go to Dairy Queen after, too, if you want."

The look on Jim's face was a sight I will never forget. He had tears streaming down his face. He knew he would never leave the hospital and he was lost for words. What could he tell his five-year-old? It was a horrible scene to witness. It was a prime example of how fucked-up and unfair life is for some.

Little Jimmy saw that his dad was crying and like most five-year-olds, would do, he just blurted out, "Why are you crying, Dad? What's wrong?" Again, no good way to answer that one. Little Jimmy then traced his dad's lips with his index finger and drew a smile on his face and forced his dad's lips upward at each corner of his mouth. That is when I had to get out of the room. It was becoming very emotional for me. I was tearing up. Who could witness such a scene and not tear up? Only a monster, I think. But I wanted to get out of there; I didn't want to add to my patient's troubles by breaking down and causing his son to worry more, as no doubt he would know that if his dad's nurse was crying, it was not a good sign.

Soon after that Jim started shutting down, both physically and emotionally. Our conversations were shorter every day. He was fading fast, and a week later he passed away. It was late at night and his son was not there, and I was glad of that as I believe he was just too young to witness such a thing, but others would disagree. At any rate he was gone, and his wife had been with him so he did not die alone. You might be surprised how many people do die alone, with no family there.

After Jim's wife had said her last goodbye, it was time for us to prep Jim for the morgue. There are a few things that we always have to do to prep a body, and when we are done, we move the body to a stretcher to take to the morgue. When we hoisted Jim's body onto the stretcher, a piece of paper had been partially underneath his chest and fell to the floor. It was the picture of him and his son fishing at their favorite place on the river. On the far side of the river, you could see the Dairy Queen. Now what does a person do at that point, laugh or cry? I did a bit of both and made sure his wife got that picture.

What happened to Jim wasn't quick and didn't involve a horrific accident and wasn't plastered on the front page of the newspaper for all to see, but it was just as hard to witness, and seeing our patients die day in and day out takes its toll on nursing staff.

Have you ever tried to lose weight? Unless you're an ectomorph, which is a skinny person who just can't seem to ever gain weight, then I'm betting you have tried to shed a few pounds at one time or another. Most Americans and those in many other countries around the world are too heavy. When I say too heavy, I mean big enough that the extra weight is putting their health at risk, and keeping them from functioning as well as they should. I, too, fall into this category. Some people become desperate and turn to all kinds of magic pills. The prospect of losing a bunch of weight without a strict diet and exercise regimen is too good to pass up for many.

In the early '90s, Ephedra pills were easy to obtain. A person could buy them at a truck stop for about $6.00 for fifty tablets, of 25 mg each. Ephedra is illegal to take for weight loss in most areas now. It is a central nervous system stimulant, and people use it because it decreases appetite, which it does quite well. But, unfortunately, it can cause heart palpitations, among other things. So, basically, you are at high risk of having heart failure if you take it, which means you can die. YOU CAN DIE—that's the main thing to take away from this.

One time, when I was working in a general hospital, we had been informed that an ambulance was coming to us with an active code in progress. That meant they were performing CPR on someone who'd had heart failure. A couple of minutes later they wheeled in a 28-year-old woman. She was quite obese, and the attendants said they suspected that she was using Ephedra as reported by her mother.

We all thought that she had likely taken too much and it had gotten out of hand. Ephedra is very effective and it does not take much to cause all kinds of deleterious effects. I have had patients who suffered from extremely low blood pressure. In fact, it was so low that they would keep passing out and falling down for no good reason, other than their blood pressure was too low. I have seen doctors order half a tablet, 12.5 mg, for a patient and their blood pressure would increase 20 or 30 points. That's a lot, very similar to what happens to a person when they smoke a cigarette. When half a tablet does that, can you imagine what happens to out-of-shape people when they take five or more tablets at a time? That is exactly what some people do. No wonder their heart stops.

We worked on this woman for a long time, trying to get her heart pumping on its own again, with no luck. She had turned purple, and her skin was mottled. She was also covered in her own feces and urine. It's really hard to describe until you see a person like this; it's just really hard to picture. We medical staff see this kind of thing a lot. What we don't always see is what I saw next. As I was performing compressions on our victim, I noticed that her mother was standing in the doorway of the emergency room with a young child in each hand. They were about four and six years of age. No child should ever see their mother looking like that, with a team of people pressing on her chest, sticking needles in her with all the monitors beeping.

Obviously, these kids would be traumatized. The fact is that when nursing staff see this type of thing, it weighs on us, too. Seeing this type of thing over and over again has a cumulative effect. Many nursing staff have PTSD, post-traumatic stress disorder, from all the dozens and dozens of traumatic situations they have had to witness. It all adds up.

Many people seem to think we are trained to handle those types of situations so they should not affect us. That's bullshit. How do you ever train to see hundreds of people die horrible deaths? What book should I buy for that? What class did I miss?

The way many people deal with trauma is by turning to alcohol or drugs. It happens a lot, a lot more than you might think. Some do therapy but usually wait until it is too late and they already have an addiction problem, are divorced, or 70 lbs overweight. Please remember there are a lot of health care workers who are also struggling to deal with the traumatic things they've seen, and will continue to have to witness in their chosen career.

Kids Shooting Kids

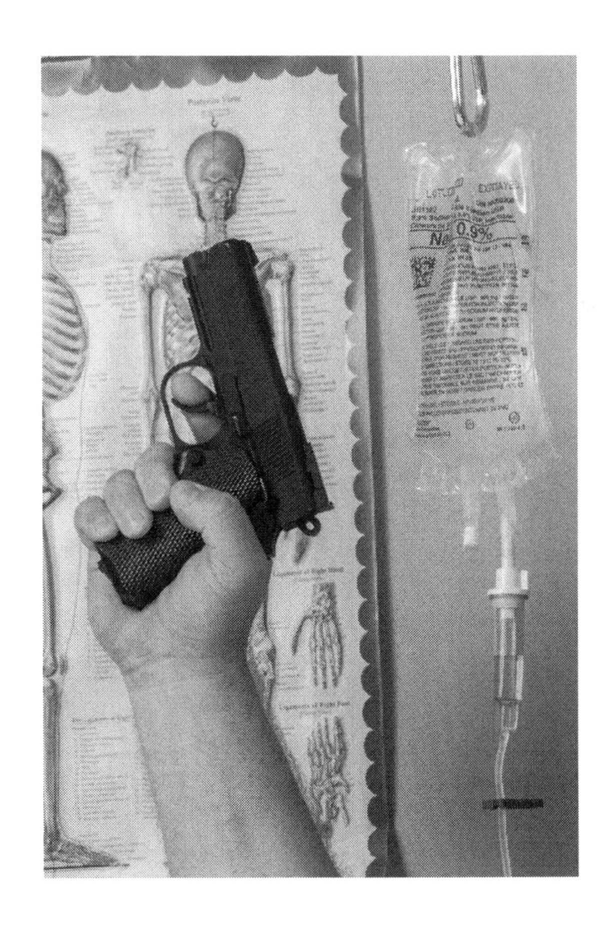

There is a lot of talk these days about shootings at schools. In fact, there are a lot of these types of incidents, and they seem to be on the rise. Many people think that lax gun laws are the problem, and others say you will never get all the guns off the streets. I have heard many a person say, "The criminals will always have guns, so honest people should be able to own guns to protect themselves." Sadly, I agree that most criminals will always own guns. I also don't think that everyday people need 14 assault rifles with three magazines each, and nine pistols. If most people own an abundance of weapons, it only makes sense that more minors will have access to them. In my experience, most gunshot victims I have worked on have been between the ages of 14 and 19. To that point, I vividly remember one night shift where this was the case.

One Saturday evening when I was working in Texas, I responded to a Code Red, in the emergency room. As I arrived in the ER, I saw many young Black men about 14 to 19 years of age, some not even men, holding pistols. They all appeared tense and ready to use them. One kid was holding a Glock as he stood beside his friend, who was laid out on his back and was not responsive. As it turned out, the kid who was covered in blood and holding a pistol wasn't angry with the staff, but he and the others were basically standing guard to make sure the rest of the other gang didn't show up and finish them off. It was a very intimidating sight to say the least. It was the first time I had to deal with gunshot victims, and actually had people with real weapons waving them around me. It was like being thrown into a live action movie, but not the least bit enjoyable to be watching.

The patient was a large man, about 6'5" and 300 lbs. He had an intravenous line started and was having fluids pumped into him as quickly as possible to make up for the huge amount of blood loss. A nurse whom I had never met waved me over and said, "Can you take this one?" and she then ran to an adjacent room to render aid to yet another of the 11 gunshot victims we now had in our ER.

This 17-year-old kid was now in my care, and mine alone, as there were not enough staff available to assist me. I went into a bit of a panic mode. I really did not know what the hell I was doing, so I just stuck with the basics: administer oxygen, fluids via IV, plug as many bullet holes as I could, and as quickly as I could. My patient was shot nine times: four bullets had entered directly into his chest cavity, two had passed through each arm, and the ninth had grazed his right side close to his liver. The wounds appeared to be made from what was most likely a 9 mm projectile. A nine-millimeter bullet makes a hole slightly smaller than the size of a dime. So, he was full of pretty big holes and was bleeding out fast. By the time he had his third bag of IV fluid in him a doctor arrived on the scene. "Thank fuck!" I said aloud, as I was about to shit myself. I really was lost as to what to do next. They never covered this shit in school—not really.

The patient was starting to gain consciousness by that time. I knew this because he called me a "fucking cracker." A "cracker" is what Black people called white people at the time.

The doctor instructed me to start a Foley catheter, and then left the room. I yelled to him, "Wait, where are you going?" Stupid question on my part; obviously he was helping other victims, too. Anyway, my next task was clear. I was thankful for that. I knew what to do; I had inserted hundreds of catheters. A catheter is basically a tube inserted into the bladder, and it would help us measure how much output of urine there was, and would tell us right away if the patient's bladder would have been nicked by a bullet, which was very important to know. If so, he could bleed out very quickly, as the bladder is very vascular.

Before I was able to put the catheter in, my patient said, "No way, Cracker; it'll hurt. Get the fuck away from me." Normally, I would be able to take more time with a patient, do some health teaching, give him a little time to think about his choices. In this case, time was critical, and I decided I had spent enough time bartering with him. Before I realized what I was doing, I blurted out, "Listen, it won't hurt your pecker any more than if you had the Dose," referring to a sexually transmitted disease. My patient stared at me for about three seconds, and then said, "Oh, okay, put it in then." Just then, I realized the hospital nursing supervisor was standing beside me. I thought to myself, *Could the fucking day get any worse? Am I going to be reprimanded for saying what I did*? To my surprise, this tough-to-please supervisor put her hand on my shoulder and said, "Good job, boy."

By this time the police had arrived, or more of them had, and they had managed to clear the room of the remainder of the gang members—the ones with all the guns. I was glad of that, as it was quite frightening. As I was setting up to put the Foley catheter in my patient, a state trooper nearly pushed me out of the way and was disrupting my sterile field in his attempt to question the patient. He was saying, "Hey boy, who shot you? Who fired the first shot? Give me your full name, your real name," stuff like that.

As this patient was barely alive, and not out of the woods by any means, I raised my voice and asked the officer to "move back out of my way, please." He ignored me. My adrenaline was probably a little high, and I found myself pushing him aside with one arm as I said, "Move, now." At that time, he did move but gave me a very angry look. He must have realized that I had a job to do, or he would have likely done more than give me an angry look. You don't touch an officer, not in Texas, without paying a price. The officer then said, as he shook his head, "I don't know why you're working so hard to save this [N-word]; he's just going to go out and shoot somebody else in six months."

Now, is it any wonder we have racial issues, when an officer talks openly like that in front of witnesses? I could only imagine how he behaved when nobody was around.

Finally, the doctor came back to save me—oh, and the patient, too. The victim had a hemothorax, which means that the bullets allowed his left lung to fill up with blood, and therefore, he was having extreme trouble breathing. That made sense; he hadn't called me a "cracker" in a while. The doctor then inserted a chest tube, which drained off about 2000 cc of blood. That would fill one of those large plastic drink bottles, the biggest ones you can buy. That's a lot of blood. The victim quickly got his breath back and was able to send more racial insults our way. This racism we have is such a vicious circle; it's pathetic and sad, yet was extremely common, given where we were. The doctor then took some lidocaine, which is used to numb an area, and squirted it on his pinky finger and began inserting his finger into each of the bullet holes—another thing you don't get taught in school. It was pretty neat to see. Lidocaine also constricts the blood vessels, which decreases some of the bleeding. Medicine can be pretty cool at times.

About six months later, I had a new neighbor move in beside me. She was a stunner, and was also a state trooper. So, naturally, I made her acquaintance right away. As we were sitting by the pool and talking about work, etc., she said, "I think I remember you from the ER." She went on to say that she was there that night of the big shoot-out. I mentioned the racial slur that the officer had made regarding my patient. She said, "Oh yeah, that's Don. He's a real asshole; nobody likes him." She then said, "But he was right about one thing, even though he said it in a horrible way. That big guy did go and shoot three people—it was just a few weeks ago. He killed two of them."

So, it turned out that the racist officer called it right, as far as the patient we saved that night did go out and shoot someone like he said he would. Obviously, the patient had been the one to decide to get another gun and go out and shoot people with it, and it was not the officer's fault. I did wonder, though, how having the patient hear the officer refer to him as the N-word and cast his prediction about how he was just going to go out and shoot someone anyway, would affect him. Talk about being labeled. We have a very long way to go with how we treat each other. I am originally from the north, and I never experienced racism like I witnessed when I lived in the south. I don't know if that patient was a bad man at his core, but there was no need for the officer to carry on like he did. Unfortunately, that was far from the last time I would witness such horrible racial abuse in my career.

Tea Time

When a person is fresh out of nursing school and starts their first job, they don't actually know much. Some of them may think they do, but in actuality, their learning is just about to begin. We learn way more skills in the first year or two on the job than we ever could in school. This is normal, as school only provides us with a good preliminary knowledge base. Because of this, most hospitals have developed a policy where a new nurse is paired up with a seasoned nurse for a few days. The experienced nurse makes sure we newbies are ready before we can be left to work on our own. I remember my first job, I was paired up with Nurse Wanda, a 55-year-old Jamaican woman with a thick accent. She was very religious, quiet, and an excellent nurse. Wanda was filled with empathy for her fellow man, top-notch as they say.

Wanda sent me into a room to do a nursing assessment on an elderly man who'd had a left-sided stroke. This assessment is routine, done every shift by a nurse for each patient. We listen to your lungs, heart rate, assess your skin integrity, circulation, and cognitive ability, etc. The list is long. Anyway, Mr. Tetley was sitting in the chair with his meal tray in front of him when I entered the room. He had dysphasia, or trouble speaking, since he'd had his stroke. His left-side extremities were also impaired due to the stroke. Mr. Tetley began saying, "Tea, tea," as I approached him. I said, "Your tea is right there," and pointed to it. He repeated, "Tea, tea." I remembered that sometimes people with a left-sided stroke don't see objects on their tray if they are on the left side of it, and if they do, they can't pick them up due to the paralysis. Therefore, nursing staff are taught to place things on the other side of the tray. I did just that. I moved the tea cup to his right side and informed him of that. But Mr. Tetley kept repeating, "Tea, tea, tea, tea, tea, tea," and seemed to become upset. It was clear to me he needed some assistance. We usually let the patient do as much for themselves as they can, and then help them when they need help. So, I decided I would help Mr. Tetley with his tea. I raised the cup to his mouth and attempted to give him a sip. He could not sip the tea; it kept running down his lips. He would not open his mouth, but began yelling in his stifled voice due to the stroke, "Tea, tea, tea, tea, tea, tea," louder and louder.

I left the room and Wanda asked how he was doing. I explained the situation to her. Partway through the story, she said, "Oh, no," and quickly went in to check on Mr. Tetley. As I followed closely behind her, I could see urine running down Mr. Tetley's leg and onto the floor.

Mr. Tetley was trying to tell me he had to pee, and I let the poor guy piss his pants. I did not know that "tee tee" was the expression people in Texas use to express their need to pee. I felt really bad and I think Wanda felt worse for me, as she had explain the situation. I soon learned that there were many different words used by people when you move many states away from where you grew up.

The very next week, Wanda and I were on the night shift. One of our patients was experiencing problems and his doctor needed to be called. I got out the patient's chart and medication sheets. We always want every bit of information at our fingertips when we call a doctor, especially in the middle of the night. They don't like to wait for nurses to find stuff when they are on the phone—I guess I wouldn't, either. Anyway, once I gathered up all the papers I needed, I said to Wanda, "Is this his real name (as I pointed to the patient's name), JESUS GONZALES?" Wanda, replied, "Yes, a lot of Mexicans have that name." I was very surprised that anyone would name their kid after Jesus Christ, the Son of God. Anyway, I called his doctor and informed him "Your patient, Mr. Jesus (Gee-zuss) Gonzales is having chest pain." The doctor paused for a couple of seconds and then said, "Let me guess, you're the fucking Yankee. It's Jesus (Hay-zeus), not Jesus (Gee-zuss)."

I was quite embarrassed. I told Wanda the story and she gasped, put her hands over her mouth and then bent over, doubled up, and began laughing very hard. Then she looked up as her eyes widened and said, "Oh, no, I think I peed a little," and took off for the bathroom. Later, she returned and said, "I don't know what I'm going to do with you. You made Mr. Tetley pee his pants and now you made me pee mine."

There were many words that I would have to learn to help me work in the South. My whole life, whenever I had to relieve myself, I did it in a toilet, but in Texas, it was a "commode." I didn't know what the hell people were talking about most of the time for the first few months, and my patients struggled to understand me. When people use the work "fixin'" it doesn't mean something is broken, but that they are about to do something. There are many words that are used differently, and it can be quite problematic when you don't know this. Just ask Mr. Tetley.

For a while, I was studying sign language. I thought it would come in handy, as deaf people get sick too. It was also fun to learn. I concentrated mostly on how to convey key words that would come up a lot at work. For example: *pain, sick, heart attack, needle, hungry, food, eat, toilet*, you get it. Anyway, I had the opportunity to use my new skills on several occasions and was feeling pretty good about myself. Other nurses would come to me if they were having trouble communicating with a deaf patient, and I was always happy to assist.

One day, we had a routine fire drill. We had to check on each patient, do a head count, shut fire doors, etc. No big deal—unless you're deaf. I went and informed our young patient who was deaf, through the use of my sign language, that we were experiencing a fire drill. He nodded and signed something, but I couldn't make it out. About 15 minutes later, after the fire drill had been completed, security called the floor and said, "I think I have one of your patients here in the parking lot. He can't talk; I think he is confused—he's standing here in only his gown, with half of his ass showing, and holding on to his IV pole." As it turned out, my poor patient misunderstood my message. He had left down the side stairs, dragging his IV down with him, as he thought the hospital was burning up. I had scared the shit out of him, and needless to say, I felt very bad and embarrassed. I definitely needed to work more on my sign language. After he had calmed down, he actually had a good laugh about it, but not me. I would feel bad all over again each time I had to enter his room after that.

Sex, drugs and chest compressions . . .

Nursing is a very difficult and demanding job—most people can appreciate this. The vast majority of nurses are hard-working, conscientious, empathetic and self-sacrificing. We all know nurses like these.

Sadly, there are some nurses—and doctors—who are simply not up to the task. Some people are just not cut out for the job and others are lazy, which results in negligence. Patients suffer because of this.

This book is a compilation of true stories from the hallowed halls of heath care, as experienced by Nurse Jack, a male registered nurse who has seen it all. From sex amongst staff and drug abuse on the job, to out-of-control patients, foul-mouthed Southern Belles and octogenarian escape artists, Jack Houston writes with humor and compassion about his years spent on the job.

The all-too-real dangers facing nursing staff, rampant racism in health care, and failures of the system to protect our most vulnerable are also explored in Houston's insightful, no-holds-barred style. If you're a fan of *ER* or *Grey's Anatomy*, you'll want to read this book. You won't believe what REALLY goes on in our hospitals.

Biography

Jack Houston was born in Ohio and raised in a small village outside of Cleveland in the Northeastern US. After graduating with an RN degree, he worked as a nurse in both the United States and Canada. Now retired, Houston lives in Ontario, Canada, during the summer and winters in Texas with his wife and two dogs.